DRAMA FOR MENTALLY
HANDICAPPED CHILDREN

HUMAN HORIZONS SERIES

DRAMA FOR MENTALLY HANDICAPPED CHILDREN

Ann B. McClintock

A CONDOR BOOK
SOUVENIR PRESS (E & A) LTD

First published 1984 by Souvenir Press (Educational & Academic) Ltd,
43 Great Russell Street, London WC1B 3PA
and simultaneously in Canada

ISBN 0 285 64981 7 casebound
ISBN 0 285 64980 9 paperback

Printed in Great Britain by
Redwood Burn Limited,
Trowbridge, Wiltshire

TO CAROL – FOR BEING HERSELF

Acknowledgements

This book would not have been written without the helpful contributions of a great many people, too numerous to mention by name. To all of them I extend my grateful thanks and acknowledge the support and help they have given me. In particular, I would like to thank the headteachers, staff and parents of Dalton, Dean Bank, Greenburn, Springhill and Victoria Park Schools for allowing me to work with their children, for providing advice and guidance, and for giving their permission to reprint photographs. A special word of thanks must go to the late Ian Henry, who gave up his free time to take the photographs printed here and to Anna Richmond who helped with the music of the songs. My thanks also to William Dunn, my research supervisor, to Glasgow University and the Scottish Education Department for grant funding, and, finally, to my long-suffering husband and patient daughter, who kept me going with cups of coffee and words of encouragement while I was writing this book.

Contents

CONTENTS

Preface

My interest in the possibility of using drama as a learning medium for mentally handicapped children was first aroused when, as a student teacher, I was sent to do some teaching practice in a primary school in the East end of Glasgow. Attached to this school was a special unit for mentally handicapped children. The staff in the unit persuaded me to come along and do some drama with the children in one of my free periods. As I knew very little about mentally handicapped children at this time, I was not at all sure how the children would react to drama or whether I would be able to work with them. But to my surprise the children responded to the work with pleasure and vigour, and my fears that they might not be able to understand how to join in drama activities were soon dispelled. Working with the children and staff was a real eye-opener for me and what surprised me was not how limited the children were, but how much they seemed to be able to understand and respond to, in spite of their handicaps.

When my stint of teaching practice in the school was over, I was unable to go on working officially with the children because at that time local authorities did not employ trained teachers to work with the more seriously mentally handicapped. However, thanks to some judicious planning by the head teacher, I was able to take up my first teaching post in a junior secondary school which catered for the needs of behaviourally disturbed and educationally handicapped teenage girls.

Since that time my career has meandered around in various branches of teaching and lecturing, but I always seemed to spend at least a part of my time working with disabled people. The more I worked with these groups, the more convinced I became that drama was a valuable learning medium for handicapped people.

The idea of writing a book on the subject occurred to me about ten years ago. At that time I was working as a part-time drama teacher in a special school. The reason I thought of writing a book was the sheer frustration I experienced when searching, often unsuccessfully, through textbooks on drama to find material suitable for my classes. Surely, I thought, there must be others who are experiencing the same difficulties? But what held me back from writing at that time was the knowledge that my own experience of teaching drama to mentally handicapped children might not be relevant to the needs of others, and that the material which I had found useful in gaining a response from the children might not suit the teaching style of others.

Some years later, however, I was fortunate in being given an opportunity to carry out research into drama with mentally handicapped children. This gave me the chance to broaden my own experience and benefit from the experience of others. In the course of my research I was able to visit many schools, to work with children with a whole range of disabilities, to collaborate with teachers and to find out at first hand from parents and teachers how drama related to the needs of their children. As a result, I became aware that many parents and teachers were keen to see drama developed as a means of stimulating their children's imagination, their social development and their communication skills. But, like myself, many of these people were having difficulty in finding material that was suitable for their children's needs.

It was in response to their prompting that this book finally came to be written. In it, I've tried to express some of my own feelings about the value, the purpose and the nature of drama in the education of mentally handicapped children. I've tried to make the suggestions in the book as practical as possible by sticking to material which has been tried and tested in the classroom or in the home. I hope that at least some of this material will prove useful to others wishing to include drama activities in the education of their mentally handicapped children.

Introduction

This book is intended primarily for use with seriously mentally handicapped children in the six to eleven or twelve-year-old age range, although many of the activities may be readily adapted for use with children younger than this. Since children within this age group can vary widely in their understanding of the spoken word and in their capacity for imaginative play, the activities suggested range from simple one-to-one games in which the child is encouraged to imitate the words and gestures of an adult, to more complex drama techniques involving play-making, dramatisation and improvisation, and through which the child can develop his imagination and learn to co-operate or interact with others.

Throughout the book an indication is given of the suitability of various techniques for different levels of ability. The book is divided into three sections. Part one gives some of the theoretical background of educational drama and, for those who have never taught drama before, gives an indication of how to determine the stage of development which children have reached in relation to different aspects of drama. In this section, there are suggestions for parents and teachers on how to start off drama in the home or school, and some of the more common problems which may be encountered are discussed in practical terms. More experienced teachers may prefer to miss out this section and go straight on to Part two. Part two gives examples of the different kinds of activity which may be tackled with children who are in the earlier stages of development or who may need to work on an individual basis with an adult. Part three deals with the more advanced drama techniques, and gives examples of material suitable for use with more able children who have better developed imaginative abilities and who can work in a group.

Most of the activities can be carried out in a relatively small space within the home or classroom, and very little in the way of special equipment is required. For many of the activities, no previous experience of drama teaching is necessary. Although the activities suggested use standard drama techniques, the actual ideas given are ones which I have developed and used in my teaching and which I have found that children responded to with interest and enthusiasm. Similarly, the anecdotes quoted are taken from real life. Only the names of the children have been changed to preserve anonymity. Throughout the book, and purely as a matter of convenience, I have referred to the child as 'he' and the adult as 'she'. No significance should be read into this!

PART ONE

The theory of drama in the education of mentally handicapped children

1 What is Educational Drama?

Most people tend to associate drama with the theatre and with plays performed on stage. Because of this, those who have had no training in drama and whose only contact with it has been in amateur theatricals or as a member of an audience, may be somewhat unsure of what is meant by drama in an educational context.

Certainly, the performance of plays or shows is an important aspect of drama, and one which can be enjoyed by children and adults alike. But performance is only one aspect of the whole spectrum of activities which go to make up drama in education. Educational drama can take many forms, depending on the needs and abilities of the child or children involved.

I say 'child or children' because, although most drama activities are generally carried out in a group, there may be quite a sizeable number of mentally handicapped children who can benefit more, in the early stages at least, from drama work carried out on a one-to-one basis with an adult. This adult may be a teacher, a parent or another member of the child's family who knows him well. Grandparents can often help here. So can older brothers and sisters. But, like everything else, drama needs to be presented fairly regularly over a period of time in order to achieve the maximum benefits from it. Whoever carries out the work, therefore, should have enough time available to work with the child on a regular basis. I have found that it can be particularly effective when parents and teachers work in co-operation with each other, with parents supplementing in the home the work the teacher does in class.

But, whether the work is carried out at home or in school, on a one-to-one basis or in a group, the principles on which the drama work is based will be the same, although the activities and the way they are presented may vary.

So what exactly is drama? What are the principles involved? And what kind of activity may be used? Rather than try to give a direct answer to these questions at this point, I should like, instead, to describe three scenes. The first scene takes place in a living room.

John and his mother are kneeling on the floor in the centre of the room. They seem to be patting at the air in front of them. Suddenly John's mother sits back and says,

'I think he's finished. Do you?'

John shakes his head. His mother looks at him and asks, 'What does he need, then?'

John points to his head.

'Ah' he says.

'A hat?' she asks, and John nods and smiles, pointing to his head.

'A hat, that's a good idea! What colour will it be?'

Seeing John's blank look, his mother quickly adds (pointing to his jumper),

'A red hat? Like your jumper? A red hat?'

John smiles and nods. 'Ed ah,' he repeats.

'Right,' says his mother, 'we'll give him a red hat. You help me to put it on him. Oh, it's very tight. Push hard. Push. That's the way. There! Now he's finished. Our snowman's finished and he's wearing a red hat. Do you like him?'

John looks at the empty space between himself and his mother, he beams and nods vigorously.

Let's leave John and his mother there for the time being

and go on to the next scene. This time it is a classroom.

> Under various desks and in corners a number of children are hiding. Some have rather frightened expressions on their faces, but most are smiling or giggling. In the middle of the room a teacher is striding up and down and saying in a loud, booming voice, 'They've got away from me this time, but they won't get away again. And if I catch them, I'll lock them all up and they'll never get away. Oh, but I'm tired. I think I'll have a rest.'
> He yawns and stretches hugely, sits on a chair in the centre of the room, and appears to fall asleep. The children creep slowly and quietly out of their hiding places. They tip-toe towards the teacher. He sneezes very loudly. The children rush back to their places. After a few minutes they begin to creep out again, led by Stephen. Stephen is one of the children who had a frightened look on his face. He beckons to the others and whispers, 'Come on, this way.' He begins to move over to the other side of the room and the other children follow him.

Again, let's leave them there and turn to our third example. Once more the scene is a classroom. And again there are a number of children in the room, but, in this case, two adults.

> One of the children, Mary, is holding a small drum and tapping gently on it with her fingers. The other children and adults are crouching down and moving around the room taking tiny steps. Mary gives the drum a much louder tap with the flat of her hand. The others all stop. One adult says, 'Good, Mary. What shall we be this time, Peter?' Peter scratches his ear and smiles, but he makes no attempt to answer. The adult prompts him. 'Big men with big feet, or little men with little feet?' Peter still doesn't answer, but several other children shout out, 'Big men.' One adult says, 'Right. We'll be big men this time. OK, Peter? Will you help us?' She takes the

drum from Mary and goes over to Peter. She helps him to hold the drum in one hand and, taking his other hand, helps him tap quite loudly on the drum as she says, 'Big men with big feet take big, big steps.' The other adult and the rest of the children join in some of the words and they all begin to take big, exaggerated steps, moving around the room.

EDUCATIONAL DRAMA

At first glance, the three scenes I have just described may not appear very similar. But there is one common factor present in each of them, which links them all, and allows them to be called educational drama. In every case, the children were being encouraged by adults to take on a role or act out an imaginary situation. So, in answer to the question – 'what is drama?' – probably the simplest reply is that *any activity which involves human beings in projecting themselves into an imaginary situation and using their voices and bodies to act out the characters and events they have imagined, may be described as drama.* Educational drama is simply the method by which adults help children to acquire skill in this process, provide opportunities for them to practise their skills, and structure and guide these activities in such a way that children learn from them.

So let us go back to our examples and see what this means in practice. In the third example the children involved were quite young – between six and seven. The role they were acting was a very simple one – a big man with big feet! In this situation the teachers were making use of very simple movement, sound and speech activities in order to teach children to recognise and say the words 'big' and 'little', and to understand something of the meaning of the words by experiencing the contrast between the two types of movement. Moreover, the adults were making sure, by giving him physical support and individual help, that Peter – the least able child in the group – was not being left out of either the fun or the learning.

The roles being played out in the second scene were much more complex – those of a giant and the people who had wandered into his castle by mistake and were trying to make their way out without being caught by him. In this case the activity was dramatisation of a story and the technique the teacher was using was that of role-play or, as it is commonly called, 'person in role'. These children were older, between ten and twelve, and they had already had some practice in group drama. They were sufficiently skilled in it to be able to carry on the dramatic action even when the teacher was not looking at them – and was, in fact, sitting with his eyes shut. Stephen was clearly behaving as the leader of the group, perhaps because he had a more developed imagination than the others. Certainly his facial expression suggested that he was finding it easy to believe in the situation and to act it out convincingly. The others appeared to be ready to accept his leadership without question.

So what were the children in this group learning from the activity? Well, in addition to learning how to act out a part, the children were learning how to behave co-operatively as part of a group and they were beginning to take personal responsibility for behaving in an appropriate and orderly way. The children had not been told how the story ended. The teacher was leaving it up to them to decide how they might get away and how to act out whatever idea they decided upon. In this case, Stephen was trying to lead them out while the giant was asleep. For the children, this was just good fun. But in the process of having fun, the children were learning how to take decisions and follow through a course of action. Stephen, in particular, was experiencing being a leader in this situation.

The teacher was able to hand over the leadership and control of the lesson to the children at this point because he had taken a role in the drama which allowed him to do so. Having done this, he had to carry out his role convincingly and trust the children to behave appropriately. However, if anything went wrong, he only had to open his eyes and once more he would be able to direct the activity in his role as giant, without having to break the dramatic action by reverting to being the teacher.

In the first example quoted, John and his mother did not appear to be playing a role at all. Mother was still mother, and the child still himself. The situation they were involved in, however, was one which required a considerable degree of imagination. Both had to imagine that the empty space in front of them contained a snowman and they had to act towards this space as if it really was a snowman! In other words, while still retaining their own life roles, John and his mother had agreed to suspend their belief in reality for a while and believe, instead, in the reality of the imaginary task they were engaged in. John and his mother were using one of the earliest forms of dramatic activity, dramatic play. By joining in his play, John's mother was able to suggest ideas which would extend his range of play behaviours and stimulate his imagination.

All the children in these examples were seriously mentally handicapped. With the exception of the 'sleeping giant', none of the adults had any special training in drama. And when I tell you that John was six years old, very seriously brain damaged from birth, epileptic and with very little speech, you will appreciate how much work must have gone into enabling him to take part in such a complex mental activity.

Indeed, this task would be almost impossible were it not for the fact that the ability to imagine, to take on a role and to act it out, appears to be naturally present in human beings from a very early age. We have not yet discovered enough about the human brain to know precisely why this should be so. What we do know is that it is a normal feature of child development for children, at about the age of three to four years, to begin spontaneously to engage in make-believe or dramatic play.

DRAMATIC PLAY

In our culture, the first attempts at make-believe are generally something like 'feeding the doll', 'putting teddy to bed', or imaginative games with toy cars. Gradually, children begin to extend this make-believe by taking a role in relation to their toys and by including other people in different roles in their play.

By using their imagination in this way, children can pretend to be anyone or anything they want to be and they can transform the here and now into any place or time they choose. They can remember and recreate for themselves past experiences, they can prepare for future events, and they can find out what it feels like to act out a role which may be quite different from their actual role in life.

This is an important step forward in development because it means that the child is now able to combine ideas and make mental associations between objects or people without necessarily having these physically present before him. Moreover, it appears that the brain development which enables the child to 'pretend' is very similar to that which enables him to combine single words in new ways to produce short phrases and sentences. So dramatic play is usually accompanied by an increase in language development. But language and thought appear to be closely related to each other, and it has been demonstrated that children who have been disadvantaged in some way and who fail to master the skills involved in this form of play, tend to have problems not only in their use and understanding of language, but also in their ability to reason and follow through a train of thought. Dramatic play, therefore, appears to be a necessary stage in the development of thinking and language.

At first, this play will be of a solitary nature. Later, the child will play alongside others and, eventually, he will begin to co-operate with other children in his play. This type of co-operation helps him to interact socially with other children and to begin to understand something of the complexities of social roles and relationships.

There is one other function which many psychologists believe that dramatic play performs. By acting out an experience which has frightened, disturbed or pleased him, a child can come to terms with, and begin to understand, the emotions involved. In his play he can express these emotions harmlessly without fear of the consequences. For example, a child who is feeling angry or aggressive may decide that 'teddy has been a bad boy' and use this as an excuse to express his anger by hitting out at the toy. A child who is upset by the arrival of a new baby in the family often acts out fantasies of this kind in dramatic play with a doll. Similarly, exciting episodes from favourite TV programmes may also be copied and the excitement recaptured by acting them out.

Thus, dramatic play appears to fulfil a number of important functions in the development process. As dramatic play is the earliest form of drama, and as all other forms of drama are simply variations on, or extensions of, this early dramatic play, it is logical to assume that drama activities will benefit children in similar ways to those which are associated with dramatic play. As a result of drama work, therefore, we should expect to see children benefiting in the areas of imagination, communication and in their social and emotional development. These, however, are general benefits. As we saw in the earlier examples, it is also possible to structure activities towards specific areas of learning in order to meet the needs of individual pupils.

In later chapters we shall look at how to plan lessons in order to meet these specific needs. But first, it is necessary to decide the stage of development which children have reached in relation to dramatic play. It is this which will determine the types of activity children are likely to be able to engage in. The next chapter deals with this and tries to answer the question, 'who can do drama?'

2 Who Can Do Drama?

At one time it was thought that brain damaged or seriously mentally handicapped children developed in a different way from those who were not handicapped. Now we know that all children go through the same stages of development in a similar way and in roughly the same order, though not necessarily at the same age. Mentally handicapped children take longer to reach each stage and there are some children who need quite a bit of help in making the transition from one stage to the next. Nevertheless, they do progress through the stages, and, given help, most children can achieve a great deal more than was expected of handicapped children just a few years ago.

However, because of his slower rate of development, the mentally handicapped child may miss out on the normal opportunities of playing with children of his own age. This, coupled with problems in communication, often means that the child gets little chance to practise the skills involved in the games of make-believe which other children enjoy. As a result, mentally handicapped children, who may be developmentally ready to join in make-believe play, do not spontaneously play in this way and need adult help in learning the skills involved. Some children, particularly those in the younger age groups, will not yet have reached the development level at which they know how to get enjoyment from acting out a role, and there may be many who do not yet understand how to use their imaginations in this way. So, with children who do not naturally play at make-believe, you have to decide whether they simply need help in learning how to engage in and enjoy dramatic play, or whether, developmentally, they would benefit more at this point from other forms of activity. I call these activities 'pre-drama activities' because they lay the foundations for dramatic play.

Before a child can engage in dramatic play he needs to have mastered certain other skills. Usually, he will be able to move around freely and physically explore his environment. He will be able to manipulate toys or other objects. He will be beginning to show that he has a sense of his own identity by recognising and responding to his own name and by showing that he can recognise and differentiate between other familiar people. He will have some awareness of the different parts of his body and will probably be able to respond to simple requests like, 'sit down, Tommy', 'clap hands', or 'wave goodbye'. Unless he has specific language problems such as those connected with autism, developmental aphasia or damage to the vocal mechanism, he will already have mastered a few words and may be able to understand quite a bit more. And he should be able to understand what is required of him and respond correctly when asked to imitate or copy your actions. At this stage the child will probably be playing with toys in which objects appear and disappear – for example, posting boxes with a hole at the top for a block to go in and one at the bottom for it to roll out of – and he may well enjoy games like hide and seek.

Children who can do most of these things are likely to be able to join in drama activities on a one-to-one basis with an adult, even if they have not begun, spontaneously, to engage in games of make-believe. Children who are already beginning to engage in dramatic play with toys or other objects, may very well be ready to join in group drama, unless they have specific behavioural problems which make it difficult to work alongside others in a group.

On the other hand, children who have not yet reached

the stage at which they have an awareness of themselves as individuals, children who can *understand* very little of what is said to them, and children who have not yet learned how to imitate the actions of another, are unlikely to understand the imaginative elements involved in drama. These are the children who may need more practice in other forms of play involving pre-drama activities. These take the form of speech and movement games designed to stimulate perception and attract attention, manipulative play with toys and other objects in order to develop fine motor control, and physical play which will help develop an awareness of the body and its individual parts.

Strictly speaking, these pre-drama activities lie outside the scope of this book, and are dealt with much more fully in a number of the other books in the present series, with which you may already be familiar. For those who are not, see p. 230 for details. However, I have included a few of these pre-drama activities in the activity section of the present book as a lead-in to some of the early imaginative and dramatic activities.

Finally, in the age range we are dealing with here, there may also be some children who either have a marked talent for acting out a role, or who clearly enjoy and understand what is involved in dramatic play. You will often find that these children are the leaders in games of make-believe and will try to get other children to join them in games of this kind at every possible opportunity. These children benefit enormously from the chances they get to extend the range and scope of their dramatic play by working with adults, or under adult guidance. You may find, too, that these children have reached the stage at which they want to show their work to others. Such children may be able to take part in short plays which can be performed before an audience of parents, friends or other children. At this stage, the plays will, almost certainly, have to be based more on movement than on words. Nevertheless children can get a great deal of pleasure from sharing and showing their work, and performances of this kind can do much to build up a child's confidence and self-esteem.

It is relatively easy to identify children who are ready to perform as they will usually let you know quite simply by asking if they may show their work to the head teacher, visitors, friends, etc., or by responding quickly and eagerly if you suggest that they should do so. Never, however, try to push a child who is shy and unwilling to do so, to perform his work in front of others. He may find it distressing and is unlikely to benefit from the experience.

Most parents and teachers will have a pretty good idea from watching their children at play which of these stages they have reached. If you are doubtful the following checklist should help you to decide where to start. Only tick 'yes' if the item represents the way the child usually behaves. When in doubt, I find it better to score low rather than high. That way, if you start with activities that are too easy, no harm will be done and you can rapidly move on to more demanding work. If, however, you start with work which is too difficult for the child, he may become bored, restless or distressed and much of the enjoyment which should be present in a drama lesson, and which will motivate him to continue to participate, will be lost.

One final point; if a child is clearly able to participate in group work he will still, almost certainly, benefit from extra opportunities for drama work at home. I know of one child like this who left his family no choice in the matter. Drama work done in school was regularly repeated at home with his parents and sisters, and *he* organised *them* and showed them what to do! As a result he made great strides in his language development. The interesting point that emerged, however, was that his young 'normal' sister was also benefiting from these sessions, but in a slightly different way. A very shy child, she rarely ventured out to play with other children. In many ways her development had already outstripped his, but in dramatic play they were able to play together as equals, each learning something from the other. As a result of playing with her brother in this way, she became much less reserved and more out-going with other children. These unexpected benefits arising out of drama work can often be just as valuable as the initial objectives you hoped to achieve.

CHECKLIST 1

If you are not sure whether your child is ready for dramatic play, fill in this checklist.

1 Can he show by smiling, gesturing, or in some other way that he recognises his own name when it is called?   Yes   No

2 Does he show that he can recognise his own reflection in a mirror?   Yes   No

3 Can he recognise, identify or point correctly to a number of people (including himself) when asked 'where's John/Daddy/Gran, etc.'?   Yes   No

4 Can he copy you when you ask him to point to different parts of his body and show him what to do – i.e: 'touch your head/arm/knee, etc.?   Yes   No

5 Can he point to parts of his body when asked to do so, but without being shown first?   Yes   No

6 Can he recognise the names of different toys, e.g. if you ask him to give you one toy from a group of toys, will he give you the correct one?   Yes   No

7 Does he play appropriately with toys?   Yes   No

8 Assuming he has no physical handicap that prevents him from

doing so, does he take an interest in his environment and move around freely at home and outdoors? (If your child is physically handicapped refer to Chapter 7.)   Yes   No

9   Can he say a few words such as 'mummy/daddy/all/gone/ta, etc.'?   Yes   No

10 Can he understand and carry out requests like 'sit down/clap hands/wave goodbye, etc.'?   Yes   No

11 Does he understand and respond to social praise such as 'good boy/clever boy/that was super, etc.'?   Yes   No

12 Will he sit with an adult and listen to a simple story or look at pictures in a book?   Yes   No

Scoring

A score of 6 or under suggests that the child is probably more likely to benefit from pre-drama activities and other forms of play. (see pp. 109–130 for suggested pre-drama activities).

A score of between 7 and 9 suggests that he may be ready to start on one-to-one early drama activities. (see pp. 131–146).

A score of 10 or over suggests that he is almost certainly ready to learn to join in one-to-one drama activities and may be ready for more advanced activities and group work. (Try checklist 2.).

CHECKLIST 2

1   Does he have a good range of gestures which he uses to make his wants known or to supplement speech?   Yes   No

2   Does he understand most of what is said to him, even if his ability to use language is limited?   Yes   No

3   Will he carry out simple requests when he is part of a group – e.g. 'all sit down/come over here/hang up your coats, etc.'?   Yes   No

4   Does he seem to enjoy listening to stories, songs, etc., both on his own and as part of a group?   Yes   No

5   Will he happily tolerate non-aggressive physical contact from adults or other children?   Yes   No

6   Will he seek out or initiate such contact?   Yes   No

7   Is he generally not aggressive (unless provoked)?   Yes   No

8   Will he play happily on his own in the company of other children?   Yes   No

9   When other children are playing with toys does he let them get on with it without trying to take the toys and disrupt their play?   Yes   No

10   When other children are playing with toys will he try to join in their play (peacefully)?   Yes   No

11   Does he sometimes play at making one toy stand for another, e.g. using a box or brick as if it were a car and with the appropriate car noises/using a box and scarf to make a bed for a doll, etc.?   Yes   No

12   Does he play games of make-believe by himself with toys?   Yes   No

13   Does he try to involve adults or other children in these games?   Yes   No

Scoring

If he scores 4 or under it is probably best to start with individual drama activities (see pp. 131–146). He may also be able to take part in group work if he has one-to-one contact with an adult in the group.

If he scores between 6 and 10 he is almost certain to be ready for group work and should have no severe behavioural problems that would make it difficult for you to work with him as part of a group (see pp. 147–172).

A child with a score of over 10 is likely to be able to take part in most forms of drama and may even enjoy taking part in simple performances. (see pp. 147–228).

3 Why Do Drama?

At the beginning of this book I mentioned some of the benefits which are likely to occur naturally as a result of increased opportunity for dramatic play. These general benefits are probably a sufficiently good reason for ensuring that drama is included as part of a child's general education. However, I also suggested that it is possible to structure lessons in order to teach specific things which may be particularly applicable to the needs of individual children. It also makes the planning of lessons much easier if you have a clear idea, in your mind, of what you want to achieve. Let me say right away, however, that neither these naturally associated benefits, nor the specific objectives you set, are likely to be achieved in a single lesson. More often it will be the result of several weeks, or even months, of regular work.

Very occasionally it can happen that a particular lesson gets very clear results. I remember one striking occasion when a child who had shown no previous indication that she understood the meaning of pretence became very animated and during her *first* drama lesson began to pretend to untie her laces and take off her shoes as part of the dramatic activity. What was so pleasing about this was that it was clear that she had suddenly understood the meaning of pretence because she was actually wearing lace-up shoes which she made no attempt to remove! Her general behaviour indicated that she was obviously ready for dramatic play and something in the lesson seemed to act as a trigger mechanism. But occasions like this are the exception rather than the rule. Most children are like Jane and take longer to respond.

Jane was an eight year-old who hated all forms of physical contact with others. Naturally, this was distressing for her parents and teachers, and both were keen to try any method that might help her overcome her aversion and accept normal contact. Various methods had previously been tried, but with little success. I was asked to take her for drama in the hope that this might work. I structured the lessons specifically towards this aspect, and her teachers, her mother and myself all worked with her regularly over a period of several weeks, but we made virtually no progress. The following week I tried an activity involving a cat and using a cat puppet as a teaching aid. This lesson was no more successful than previous lessons had been until the very end when Jane spontaneously took hold of the hand that held the puppet and allowed me to lead her back to the classroom. There was no sudden, dramatic improvement in her behaviour, but this incident was the turning point in our relationship and, very gradually, she began to accept contact. By the end of six months we were able to take it in turns to be sad cats (who needed to be stroked and loved) or fierce cats (tigers) who could only be tamed if someone rode on their backs. By the end of the year Jane was much more able to accept physical contact without flinching away and, very occasionally, she would spontaneously hug her parents, teachers or myself. I would not like to claim that the drama work *caused* this improvement. It was a gradual process which occurred as a result of a number of people working together to help her in a variety of ways. But I can say with certainty that drama *helped*.

So I am not claiming that drama will bring sudden benefits, except in very rare cases. If, however, drama is carried out regularly over a period of time – say three months – and you structure lessons towards specific areas of need, then there is a very good chance that the work you do in drama will go some way towards meeting those needs. In addition, drama activities can be used as a means of supplementing and reinforcing learning which has been introduced by other methods in other situations. So let's take a closer look at how to structure lessons to meet specific needs.

COMMUNICATION SKILLS

One of the most common educational problems in mentally handicapped children is the difficulty they experience in communicating. Many children have delayed speech, some find it difficult to understand the spoken word, and there are others who have very specific language difficulties which make the whole business of communication an unpleasant and frustrating experience. These communication difficulties can give rise to secondary problems arising out of the frustrations which children can experience when they cannot make their wants or needs known. Because of this, many children will already be involved in a planned programme of language development. These language development programmes use a variety of approaches, but one of the most common is one which cuts out all unnecessary words in a teaching situation and concentrates on the specific target words being taught. As the child masters one word, or one set of words, he is introduced to new words and encouraged to combine known words to make phrases and, later, sentences.

Drama work cannot take the place of these language development programmes, but drama activities can be used to supplement them in a number of important ways.

First, drama activities can make use of the vocabulary range that the child is already working on introducing the same words in a variety of different, naturalistic settings, and using normal conversational speech. For example – the understanding of prepositions like 'in' or 'out' can be increased by miming the actions of 'putting *in* and taking *out* groceries from a basket' as part of dramatic play involving shopping; children can be encouraged to jump *in* and *out* of waves on the shore as part of imaginative movement work, and in simple dramatisation of stories etc. they can pretend to get dressed to go *out* on a wet day, and take off wet clothes when they come *in*. In this way the child gets used to hearing the same words used in slightly different ways and can increase the range of associations he can make with any one word. Thus many specific items of vocabulary can be reinforced and generalised using very simple drama techniques.

Secondly, drama can be used to help counteract negative attitudes to the making of sounds which may have occurred as a result of difficulty or frustration. Some children have got into the habit of 'opting out' of making sounds simply for pleasure, because in the past they have found it difficult. Many language development programmes try to reverse these attitudes by rewarding the child with praise and a piece of some favourite food when he does try to speak. This teaches him to associate speech with pleasure rather than difficulty. Drama can have exactly the same effect, but in a slightly different way. It is unlikely that you will use real rewards very often in a drama lesson, although you will almost certainly use rewards such as expressions of praise or pleasure. But the main rewards that children get from drama tend to be those of satisfaction at being able to play in this way, and pleasure in joining in something they enjoy either with other children or with the undivided attention of an adult who also seems to be enjoying herself. Because drama is a natural part of a child's development, most children do thoroughly enjoy it, and, providing it is reasonably well taught, drama should be fun. If you can choose a subject which you know the child is interested in, or something he already likes to do, you can introduce 'nonsense' sounds as part of a drama activity based on these interests. For example, in the early stages children probably enjoy movement more than words. If you can encourage children to mime the movement of familiar activities, sounds can be used as an accompaniment to the movement. Pretending to wash hands can be made into a game by introducing simple phrases like 'turn on the hot tap. Sh. Now feel the water. Ouch! It's too hot. Turn on the cold tap. Sh. Now feel the water. Ouch! It's too cold. More hot, Shh, etc.' Similarly, if children are pretending to bounce like balls, you bounce with them, exaggerating all the movements and adding silly words like 'boing' and 'bonk' as you do so. This adds to the fun for children and they begin to take pleasure in *hearing* sounds and differentiating between them.

In lessons like this do not ask the children to join in the sounds or words. With children who are really reluctant to use their voices this may have the effect of making them even more unwilling. Simply introduce the sounds yourself as part of the fun. Eventually the children may join in of their own accord and when this does happen they are well on the way to enjoying the making of sounds for their own sake. In my experience there are few children indeed who do not respond to this method.

The same approach may be used with repetitive rhymes and in stories where there are animal noises or the sounds of cars, rain dropping, doors banging, etc. Usually children will join in with these words or sounds, but probably without a great deal of understanding at first. This does not matter. What you are trying to establish at this stage is that making sounds and words is not always a difficult and unrewarding process.

Thirdly, drama work is ideally suited to extending a child's range of natural gesture. We all use gesture to supplement our speech. Often we reply to questions simply by a shrug or a nod of the head. Children who can understand speech quite well, but who have problems in using language may have to rely quite heavily on gesture to get their meaning across. Some children do this most effectively. Others may need help in learning how they can supplement speech with gesture. Drama lessons which concentrate on improving children's ability to 'talk with their hands and bodies' can often help them communicate more freely. At first, these lessons will probably be based on exaggerated, expansive movements such as beckoning to someone, being a traffic policeman giving large, clear signals, or occupational mimes involving hammering, sawing, rocking a baby to sleep, patting a large dog, etc. Gradually the movements can be made finer until children can mime, with a fair degree of accuracy, the intricate movements involved in, for example, the threading of a needle, pouring out a glass of fruit juice, undoing the knots in the string round a parcel, etc. This will not necessarily help children to use language, but it can get them out of difficulties and enable them to make themselves understood while they are still in the process of learning to use language.

Finally, communication is not simply about making known our needs or wants. It is a means of making contact with other people. But in order to do this children need something to talk about. As adults, you know how difficult it can be to make conversation with someone when neither of you has anything of real interest or importance to say to the other. The same applies to children. Unless children have something they really want to talk about, it may simply not be worth the effort of trying to speak. In my own work the most common effect of drama on the communication process which I have noticed is that children seem to *want* to talk about it afterwards. The subject of the lesson – the story, poem, situation, etc. – provides a topic for conversation and the fact that they have been physically involved in acting out this subject seems to make it more real and they want to talk about the experience.

Certain activities like dramatisation can help children to re-tell the experience in a more logical and orderly way because it helps them to understand the sequence of cause and effect. For example, read the following two sentences:

Because he ate too many cakes the man became very fat.
The man became very fat because he ate too many cakes.

Both mean the same, and, in *telling* a story it probably does not matter too much which version you use. In acting out, however, you will want to make it clear *why* the man became fat. Therefore, logically, the eating of the cakes has to precede the getting fat. Similarly, acquiring the cakes – by buying, baking, taking them out of the cupboard, etc. – has to precede the eating. By acting out events in this logical way, children learn to understand the link between cause and effect, and this seems to help them order their thoughts logically when it comes to talking about the activity. Moreover, because children use a more logical sequence in talking about the activity and, usually, supplement this by the gestures they have already practised, the listener is in a much better position to understand and make sense of what they are saying. This, in turn, makes it more likely that the listener will respond in an appropriate way to what they are saying. The fact that the listener can understand and react appropriately is rewarding for the child and makes it more likely that he will try to communicate on other occasions. When a child learns that he can communicate not just his needs, but also his interests, his use of language in conversation will probably increase quite markedly. Let me give you an example of this. In one school a teacher had told a story involving an elderly couple who went to feed the ducks in the park. The story was acted out by the children in class. On the following day one girl, who was normally very reticent about speaking, produced a picture which she gave to the teacher, telling her that it had been drawn by her elder sister. There was no way that the sister could have known that the elderly couple were dressed in brown, that the man smoked a pipe, that the park bench was red or that there were exactly three ducks on the pond in the story. And yet all these details were present in the picture. It turned out that the child had been so keen to convey the information that she had acted out at home, for her parents and elder sister, all the activities done in class. This gave her sister an idea of what to put in the picture and she was able to get the other details by asking questions. This is not an unusual reaction to drama work and it is fairly common to find that children try hard to communicate about drama in this way.

So, although drama is no substitute for a planned programme of language development, it is a very useful method of extending a child's ability and skills in communication.

SOCIAL SKILLS

Another common difficulty experienced by mentally handicapped children is that of making social relationships and behaving appropriately in social situations. Some children may be aggressive or destructive, while others can be either hyperactive, passive or withdrawn. It is not clear in any one case how many of these behavioural difficulties are the result of the child's handicap, and how many are due to secondary difficulties arising out of communication problems or experiences children may have had of being laughed at, misunderstood or rejected by other children or adults. Whatever the cause, these problems can be difficult to deal with. Children who are very seriously disturbed will need specialised help. And in fact there are certain forms of drama – such as psychodrama and dramatherapy – which are now increasingly being used by psychologists and therapists to help children overcome severe problems. These specialist forms of drama lie outside the scope of this book. But ordinary drama activities can be structured to help children whose problems are less severe.

Any form of work in which children are encouraged to work in pairs with either another child or an adult can help teach children to co-operate. A group situation, in which each child's contribution is necessary to the success of the whole, also helps encourage active co-operation. Also children who have a tendency towards aggression can be encouraged in a group to take a role which allows them some scope for physical action and yet keeps them slightly apart from other children who might accidentally trigger the aggression. For example, in a group drama involving something as simple as children playing ball in a park, the teacher could suggest that she and the aggressive child be the park keepers who come to help the others retrieve a ball which has got stuck in a tree. The teacher can stay close to the problem child in this way without appearing to be controlling his behaviour too closely. Moreover, by giving the child a fairly prominent part in the drama the teacher ensures that he gets attention without having to attract it by aggression. Because the teacher is physically close to the child in her role as his partner any sign of aggression can be detected and dealt with before it becomes a problem simply by temporarily moving their part in the dramatic action away from the others. In this way the child is learning to tolerate being with other children in an activity and he may eventually learn how to play alongside others, or even with others, without aggression.

In individual work an aggressive child can be helped to act out some of his aggression harmlessly in forceful physical movements which are coupled with co-operation – for example, getting him to help you mime pushing a very heavy box, to lift a heavy weight, saw down trees, mime a tug of war, etc. When children are willing to co-operate in these more boisterous movements, contrast these with, for example, scenes involving workmen carrying a big pane of glass, a very precious glass ornament or a new pet kitten, etc. By contrasting forceful and delicate situations, and by working together as a team, you are encouraging the child to understand that he can be both strong and careful. Again, the extra attention he gets when he is doing so may help reduce his tendency to be aggressive or destructive.

Passive or withdrawn children need a very different approach. Asking, or trying to encourage a child to join in does not work well because it can have the effect of focusing attention on the problem. Sometimes a withdrawn child will join in group drama with others if he feels he is not particularly noticed and if others appear to be enjoying themselves. And this can generalise to other group activities. This, however, is a rather negative approach to the problem.

A more positive way is to use an activity such as puppetry. The adult can speak through, and to, the puppet and a child will often respond as if the puppet were real. Withdrawn children will often speak as the puppet because the puppet serves the purpose of diverting attention away from the child himself.

Another rather unorthodox approach, which I have found useful in individual work with withdrawn children who are at the very early stages of dramatic play, is to sit near a child without talking to him or trying to involve him in any way. Instead, I take a doll or a teddy and talk directly to it, saying a rhyme, telling a story or acting as though the toy were whispering to me, and I answer appropriately. It can feel rather awkward behaving like this, but I try to give every indication that I am enjoying myself thoroughly. Sometimes a child will be attracted and will come closer and try to join in. If he doesn't, I continue in this way until the activity is finished and then say something like, 'all right teddy, we'll have to stop playing now. You want to go to bed? OK. I'll put you to bed now. Goodnight teddy.' Having done this I simply revert to normal behaviour and carry on as though the incident had not occurred. If this process is repeated on a number of occasions, I often find that a child's curiosity is aroused, he becomes interested in what I am doing and eventually joins in without realising it. Once you have attracted a child's attention in this way, it is possible to introduce activities which will encourage him to co-operate with you and reduce his passivity.

Finally, one of the most important ways in which drama can be used to help children develop social skills is the possibilities that it holds for rehearsing future events.

Many children appear to behave badly in social situations either because they are afraid or because they have not yet learned what the appropriate behaviour is. Situations such as a visit to the doctor or dentist are obvious candidates for acting out because they are naturally frightening and the child needs to know what to expect. But less obvious situations can be frightening and can cause problems. For example, one mother had problems whenever she had to take her child on an outing by public transport bus. The school bus was accepted by the child, but, for some reason, public transport buses frightened her and she would either cry throughout the journey or throw a tantrum and refuse to enter the bus. Her mother devised some ingenious drama activities at home in order to lessen her fear. At first she simply introduced songs like 'the wheels on the bus go round and round', and a version of 'here we go round the mulberry bush' to the words 'this is the way we go to town, go to town, go to town, this is the way we go to town, in a big red bus.' They acted out situations in which they went to places, such as the seaside, in a bus. Strangely enough, the child was quite happy to do this. Eventually her mother introduced a tape of bus noises to go with these play situations. It took some time before the child lost her fear of buses, but it did go. I have used a similar approach successfully with a child who had a fear of dogs.

But it is not only frightening or threatening situations that can be acted out. Any new, or fairly unusual activity, such as shopping for new shoes, going out to a restaurant for a meal, attending a birthday party, etc. can be acted out in advance and the child can learn what to expect, and, perhaps just as important, what is expected of him. Moreover, the pleasure of a family outing such as a visit to the zoo, the circus or the beach, can be enhanced if the child has already some idea of the things he may find there. By acting out some of the possible events or objects he may encounter he is becoming more familiar with the words that may be used during the actual event, and may take more interest in looking out for the things which he has already experienced in play.

Problems in communication and social behaviour tend to be among the common areas of difficulty for children in the younger age groups. With slightly older children, or with children who have a good understanding of dramatic play, drama work can be structured more towards developing the ability to take decisions, to think out the solution to problems, or simply as a means of extending their experience of the world around them by introducing them to situations that they have not encountered in real life. With children under 10, I find that it is better to stick fairly closely to reality in these situations and to work on making the ordinary exciting and interesting, rather than looking for unexpected twists in the story or very fantastic characters and settings. Try to make use of chance events like a fall of snow, a dog straying into the garden, or the TV breaking down, etc. All of these provide potential subjects for acting and, because they are based on reality, can stimulate children to take an interest in life around them.

Finally, I can see no reason why some drama activities should not be structured simply towards fun. I certainly find that including 'fun sessions' every now and again prevents me from becoming stale and helps me enjoy my work more. For the children such sessions can provide an opportunity for laughter – which is, after all, another basic human need.

4 Parents as Teachers

Parents reading this book will know, better than anyone, just how much time is taken up in caring for a mentally handicapped child. All parents tend to be anxious that their children should have every chance to develop all the skills and abilities of which they may be capable, and most parents are only too willing to try out any activities which may help their child's development. But, while parents may be keen to try out drama work at home with their children, they may wonder, quite understandably, how to fit regular drama activities into an already busy day. Some parents, especially those who have had no previous experience of drama, may also wonder whether they have the necessary teaching skills to undertake this work. Others may wonder what problems might crop up and how to deal with these. So, in this chapter, let's take a closer look at some of the factors involved when parents take on a teaching role in drama.

THE TIME INVOLVED

Right at the beginning of this book I suggested that, like everything else you do with your handicapped child, drama needs to be carried out regularly and systematically for maximum benefit. However, this does not mean that the drama work you do with your child will need to take up a large amount of time. Rather the opposite, in fact, because short drama lessons can be just as effective as longer ones, and for children in the early stages of dramatic play it can be a positive advantage to keep lessons short. This is because, while most children can enjoy drama work, they do need to concentrate while they are doing it and there will be many children who will not be able to sustain this concentration for long periods. Moreover, in drama work children are using up physical as well as mental energy and, although they may not notice it at the time, they can become quite tired after a drama session.

Adults, too, can find lessons tiring because of the energy they need to expend in making the experience lively and enjoyable for the child. As a rough guide to the time involved, therefore, I suggest that a *maximum* of twenty minutes is quite long enough for most children at one time. For children in the early stages of the work, as little as five to ten minutes may be as much as the child is able to cope with. Many of the activities suggested in this book for children in these early stages are deliberately short and contain only one central idea. This should avoid the problem of children losing concentration and becoming bored.

Moreover, 'regular' drama work does not mean that the work has to be carried out every single day. Twice or three times a week is probably ample for most children. In fact, I find that this is better than trying to fit in a lesson every day as it gives the child a chance to think over and talk about some of the ideas presented in the previous session before moving on to the next. It also gives you a chance to assess how much of the previous session's work the child has understood and remembered, and gives you a guide as to how fast you can proceed with the work. Some children may need to have the same activities repeated on several occasions before they really understand and respond, while others may be able to work at a faster pace.

WHEN TO CARRY OUT THE WORK

Exactly when you decide to carry out the regular sessions will obviously depend greatly on your own normal household routine, but it is better if you can manage to fit the lessons in at approximately the same time on each occasion. In this way you are establishing a routine and your child gets to know that these are 'special' play-times when he will have your undivided attention. He will also begin to realise that in these play sessions you play at being different things, rather than playing with toys.

When your child is responding to the drama work and enjoying it, you will probably notice that he becomes lively or excited during the session. This is a perfectly natural and normal part of drama work, and one which is to be welcomed as a sign that your child is making progress in his understanding of the use of imagination. Moreover, this liveliness seems to be partly responsible for the increase in the enjoyment and use of language which often happens after a lesson. For the child who is naturally lethargic and passive, the stimulation of drama work can arouse his interest, hold his attention and encourage him to be more active and responsive. But a lively, excited child is unlikely to go off to bed easily and quietly. Even if you can encourage him to do so, he may be tired but too excited for sleep, and that can create problems for the whole household. So I would suggest that the one time of day which is not really suitable for drama is the late evening, just before his bedtime. The bedtime story, however, can be a useful way of introducing the child to events and ideas which can be acted out on other occasions.

Similarly, bath-time can provide the natural opportunity to introduce a gentle, imaginative element into simple water play, while still allowing sufficient time after his bath for him to calm down before bedtime. By encouraging your child to listen to the sounds of the taps or shower running, to the swish of the water as you move your hands in the bath, or to the sounds the water makes as the bath empties, you are increasing his awareness of the differences in these sounds and can help him to accompany them with appropriate vocal sounds. A simple rhyme, such as the following, can also be helpful.

When we move our hands in water
We hear – swish, swish, swish.
   (*slow swishing movements of the hands*)
When we take them out of water,
All we hear is this.
   (*Encourage him to listen to the 'silence'*)

Children generally enjoy this bath-time activity, and the associations they are making between the real and the vocal sounds can provide a useful lead-in to more imaginative work in the regular drama sessions.

Whatever time of day you choose to carry out the regular drama work, it is a good idea to finish off each session with a 'calming' activity. This should be built into the content and structure of the lesson and should occur as a natural ending to the lesson. For example, if you have been using movement as the basis for the lesson, try to ensure that you finish the lesson with a gentle movement which gradually slows down until your child becomes quite still. These moments of stillness allow the child to 'wind down' and relax after the livelier, more boisterous part of the lesson.

With children who have a tendency to become over-excited, or who are naturally hyperactive, it may also be necessary to include some of these moments of stillness in the course of the lesson in order to teach him to control his movements and regulate his activity. Moreover, recent research has shown that some mentally handicapped children suffer from a degree of deafness so slight that it is difficult to detect by ordinary screening methods, but which can lead to the child experiencing difficulty in distinguishing between letters which sound very similar such as 'p' and 'b', 't' and 'd', 'm' and 'n', etc. Sometimes these children display very restless behaviour patterns, as do some Down's syndrome children who suffer from occasional or intermittent hearing loss. It has been found that simply encouraging these children to be still and listen attentively to very soft sounds can often help them to distinguish between these sounds more effectively.

Incidentally, if your child suffers from a more severe hearing difficulty, some of the rhythmic sound, movement and mime activities suggested on p. 131 may prove enjoyable for him, and if you use large, natural gestures as well, this may help your child to respond to sounds.

Sometimes children enjoy drama sessions so much that they are reluctant for the sessions to end. Obviously it is very rewarding for the adult when this happens. But, as I said before, drama can be tiring for both the adult and child and it is better to stop while both are still enjoying the activity than to continue until one or other becomes over-tired. In any case, if the lesson stops while your child is still enjoying the work there is a much better chance that he will be eager to participate in it again and this makes starting off the next session a much easier task for you. I have found that the calming down period at the end of a lesson is quickly accepted by children as an indication that the lesson is about to end, and most children will accept this with good grace if they know that they can return to the work another day.

In a series of lessons that I developed recently I had the two central characters, who appeared in every story, coming home at the end of each 'adventure' and settling down to rest with a nice cup of tea. After this they stretched and yawned and fell asleep for a few moments. This may sound contrived, but it was a useful device in helping the children to understand that the lesson was over for that day and, after a few sessions, the children actually began to anticipate the ending and look forward to the part of the acting when they could pretend to fall asleep. Since some of these children were hyperactive, this was a useful way of settling them down before they began another, less active pursuit.

WHO SHOULD CARRY OUT THE WORK?
Which parent carries out the regular drama work will obviously depend on who has the most time available,

who is the most interested in this form of work and, perhaps, on which parent has the most skill in making imaginative activites lively and interesting. To begin with, however, it is probably better if only *one* person carries out the work on a regular basis. This helps to establish a routine from the start, and helps give your child a sense of security because there will be a degree of consistency in the type of language used, the tone of voice and the teaching style adopted. This is particularly important with children who may be at an early developmental level, or with children who have very poor concentration and find it difficult to attend to any one thing for any length of time.

As your child becomes more familiar with what is involved in this work, when he has learned to focus his attention, and particularly when he has established the ability to take on and act out a role with one person in a variety of situations, it should be possible to introduce other people into the work or to ask others to take turns in presenting the lessons and participating in the play. Through this, your child will gradually learn how to interact with a variety of people in an imaginative situation and be able to respond to those who use a different style of language or presentation. Very often grandparents or other children will be happy to lend a hand here and this can provide a welcome change in routine for you and your child.

For the more mature child, or the child who already has group drama in school, it is unnecessary to restrict the work to individual sessions. For these children, drama sessions can be occasions when, for a short time, the whole family plays together. Incidentally, such sessions can provide an opportunity for practising some of the games and activities which you might wish to provide at a birthday party for either your handicapped child or another child in the family. I mention this as one parent I knew dreaded the thought of having a birthday party for her younger daughter because her handicapped son's behaviour was very unpredictable and liable to create havoc in the games. Before her daughter's sixth birthday party the mother practised games like 'the farmer's in his den', 'here we go round the mulberry bush' and 'I sent a letter to my love and on the way I dropped it' over and over with her son until he was able to join in without too much difficulty. This meant that he was able to join in at least some of the games and, during the more complicated games, she kept him busy with a balloon pump blowing up balloons. This is one practical example of drama work being useful in a way which, as a teacher, I would never have thought of. I have no doubt that there are many other uses which individual parents will discover for themselves in the course of the work.

PARENTS' CONTRIBUTION TO THE WORK

At one time the prevalent attitude in educational circles was that the teacher 'knew best' in all matters concerning the education of children, since she was the person with the training and qualifications to do the work. Over the years this attitude has changed and it is now recognised that parents can do much to help in the education of their own children. This does not downgrade the work of the teacher. On the contrary, the teacher, precisely because of her special training, will, almost certainly, still know how best to provide a balanced programme of education and training, and how to devise the appropriate methods for teaching this in the classroom. Parents, however, can help and support the teacher in this work by communicating with her and enabling her to learn more about the personality and special interests of the individual children in her care. While the teacher, in turn, can suggest to parents ways in which they could help to supplement the work she does in class by carrying out complementary work in the home. As a parent and teacher myself, I know that, in practice, this ideal is not always achieved. Nevertheless, in special schools the numbers are small and the problems many, and for this reason alone, there does tend to be more contact between parents and teachers. In my experience there is generally a good relationship between the two, with both having the best interests of the child uppermost in their minds. This makes it easier for the two to co-operate in the development of programmes of work for individual children.

This being so, if your child is already having regular drama work at school, you will probably be aware of this either from what your child has told you or from direct communication with the teacher. In such a situation, the work you do at home with your child will be a means of extending and increasing his opportunities for dramatic play and of making up for the fact that he may not be able to go out to play with other children as frequently as non-handicapped children of his own age might do. If you can have a word with the teacher and arrange that the activities you provide will supplement the work she does in class, your child's learning will be reinforced and he should progress faster in his development of language, movement and imaginative play. For example, if the teacher is working on a programme of vocabulary training, you can make use of the words in this programme as part of the dramatic play you engage in with your child. If the teacher is working on a specific theme, you can help by providing activities that are based on or around this theme. Moreover, there is an opportunity for you to create opportunities to practise in play the ordinary, everyday activities that occur in or around the family and help your child relate these to the kind of play activities he may use at school in learning within the house or shop corner. Even if there is some duplication in this work, this ought to be no cause for concern since mentally handicapped children need opportunities to practise all their skills, and to practise them regularly, so that they do not forget the skills they have learned in the past when confronted with new skills to master. Drama is one subject in which it is relatively easy to combine new and older skills because the activities can be set within a context of everyday experience in which the familiar and the less familiar, or the forgotten, can be integrated quite naturally.

If your child is not having regular drama work in school, it may be even more important that you provide him with opportunities in the home to develop and practise his imaginative skills. With the younger child who is not yet at school, some time spent in pre-drama activities will help lay the foundation for the development of these skills and should make the task of the teacher relatively easier when he does go to school. It is in both these situations that you may well want to carry out a structured programme of work along the lines suggested in this book, and with the special needs and interests of your own child in mind. Since you cannot, in this situation, take your cue from the teacher and develop lessons which will complement her work, it is probably best to start with activities or subjects which, from your own experience, you know your child is already familiar with or interested in. Unlike the teacher who has to balance the needs of an individual child against the needs of the whole group of children in her care, parents can concentrate their attention, for the duration of the activity, exclusively on the needs of their own child, and there are few children indeed who do not benefit from short periods of undivided individual attention. The genuine pleasure which parents generally feel when they see their child enjoying himself or making progress, can communicate itself to the child, making him feel good and encouraging him to repeat the acts which so pleased his parents. Again, this can lead to faster progress in his development.

So, whether or not your child is having drama at school, you can, as a parent, make a specific contribution which may help your child to develop his skills in this area more quickly, or more effectively, than he might have done without your help and guidance. There is one other contribution which parents can make, and here I should like to address myself specifically to the parents of Down's syndrome children.

I have found from working with Down's children, that there are a number of them who are remarkably good mimics, and there are some who have good speech and who can act out a role almost as well as non-handicapped children of the same developmental age. This ability is not shown by all Down's children, nor is it only Down's children who display it. But, in my experience, this ability does tend to be found in those Down's children who have friendly, outgoing personalities and who also have a good ear for rhythmic music. Such children seem to be capable of imitating the speech, movement patterns and the facial expressions of others with little difficulty, and they seem to take a delight in doing so.

This can be a mixed blessing in that a child may be quite indiscriminating in who or what he chooses to mimic, and this can, on occasion, lead to embarrassment if the child mimics someone in an inappropriate situation. It can also create other, less obvious, problems. For example, I know one Down's child, Alan, whose speech can be either perfectly clear or relatively unintelligible depending on the time of year. In term time, when he is in close contact with his friend who has very severe problems in articulation, Alan mimics his friend with the result that his own speech deteriorates. In the school holidays when he is mainly with his family and neighbourhood children, his articulation improves markedly. In this situation, his parents believe it to be morally wrong to limit his friendship and are prepared to accept the consequences of this. They are aware, however, that a child like Alan needs, even more perhaps than other children, an outlet for demonstrating his natural ability and they have encouraged him to use this in socially acceptable ways by, for example, giving him a toy guitar which he uses to mime to 'Top of the Pops'. Such a child needs opportunities to copy adult models and, in interacting with adults in dramatic play, to extend his natural skills and learn the behaviour which is appropriate under various social conditions.

One of the unfortunate facts of mental handicap is that it limits the number of recreational interests and activities open to the child when he becomes an adult. In various parts of the country a few amateur drama clubs are now being set up for adult handicapped people. At present, these mainly cater for those with physical rather than mental handicaps. It is likely, however, that with the growing trend towards providing equality of opportunity for the mentally handicapped person, such groups will, in the future, be able to include those mentally handicapped people who have skills in this area. If your child's ability has been fostered throughout his childhood, he should, in later life, be capable of taking part in such a group and should enjoy doing so. This will provide him with both a valuable recreational interest and an opportunity to mix with others who share this interest.

Finally, such children are often as keen on *watching* drama being performed as they are on participating in it, and it does seem to stimulate their flow of language and speech. They can be attentive members of an audience, providing the play being performed is suitable for their level of experience and understanding. If you have already noted in your child a natural ability to mimic, and if you think that he could sit through a public performance without unduly disturbing those around him, try to find out about local performances of plays for children and take him along. This will encourage his interest in seeing plays performed and will help him learn how to behave appropriately as part of an audience. To be utterly realistic, he may never fully understand all the nuances and full meaning of what he hears and sees on stage, but the experience may be sufficiently meaningful for him to enjoy it and to allow those around him to enjoy it also. If he can learn how to behave in the theatre, this, coupled with his natural interest in drama, may also provide a source of recreation for him in the future.

WHAT SKILLS ARE REQUIRED?
Like any other form of teaching, the teaching of drama requires certain skills. Many of these skills are ones which

are common to all forms of teaching, and, as parents of a handicapped child you may well have acquired some of these skills already. For example, most parents will probably have developed fairly keen powers of observation and will be able to detect, and respond to, any indication, however small, that a child is making progress. By noticing and praising these you are increasing the likelihoold that your child will respond in similar ways on another occasion. Secondly, you will probably be aware of the need to catch and hold your child's attention before talking to him, and of the necessity for using clear, simple speech and language when doing so. Thirdly, you will, almost certainly, have developed the knack of breaking more complex tasks down into simple stages, and will have the patience to repeat these as often as is necessary for your child to master them.

With these skills, you are already half-way towards being able to plan and present a drama lesson. The other skills needed are the ability to make flexible use of voice, gesture and movement in presenting material, and the ability to be uninhibited in doing so, in order that your own acting can clearly convey the meanings you are trying to get across to your child. With mentally handicapped children who may have additional physical problems, such as poor hearing, poor co-ordination or poor eyesight, it is particularly important to make all movements, gestures and sounds used as clear and unambiguous as possible. With such children, and with children in the early developmental stages, it may not be enough simply to *ask* your child, for example, to 'curl up like a cat' or 'to be a cat'. You may have to *show* him what you mean by demonstrating the movements involved and by helping him to move his limbs into the appropriate positions. Similarly, the 'miaow' which accompanies this has to sound as genuine as possible if your child is going to understand and respond. In other words, everything you do has to be sufficiently 'cat-like' for your child to build up a picture in sound and movement of what it is he is being asked to represent.

Exactly the same principle applies when, for example, you are miming the actions involved in simple, everyday activities, but the actual movements you use may need to be larger than life in order to present a clear and convincing demonstration of the real movements. Similarly, if you are presenting a story it may be necessary to exaggerate specific features in the voices of the characters in order to differentiate between them and the pitch and tone of your own normal voice. For example, in a well known story like 'The Three Little Pigs' there is an obvious need for at least three different types of voice in order to establish the differences between the gruffness of the wolf, the 'grunty' or 'squeaky' voices of the pigs and the normal voice of the narrator. Individual sounds, too, may need to be exaggerated or intensified, with loud and soft sounds, short and long sounds, being clearly contrasted with each other so as to establish the different qualities in each. Thus, for example, a gentle trickle of water might be conveyed by a soft, prolonged 'ssss', while a sudden gush of water from a tap would require the much stronger, more forceful and shorter sound 'sh'.

The ability to make use of a wide range of vocal patterns, gestures and physical movements, is one which comes quite naturally to some people and they do not have to think too much about it. Others may find that acting out a role or presenting a movement or sound sequence is not something which comes easily and they may feel awkward, embarrassed or selfconscious when they first try it. Most people, however, find that they are considerably less self-conscious when alone with a child, than in situations where there is another adult present. This is another reason for suggesting that, in the early stages of drama work, it is best if only one person carries out the work with the child. If you can choose a time when you can be alone with your child, free from interruptions, and a place where you cannot be overlooked or overheard, this should help you feel less inhibited in the presentation of dramatic stimulus. Later, when you have had a chance to develop more confidence in your skills, you may be less self-conscious about being observed. You may even discover in yourself a few hidden dramatic talents which you did not know you possessed.

But even people who do not possess a natural or obvious talent for drama, will find that it is considerably easier to adopt and act out a role convincingly if they are, themselves, convinced of the reality of what they are doing. For example, if you can imagine, for a time, that you really *are* a little lost dog, you will find it easier to adopt the appropriate movements and sounds to express this. Moreover, you may find, as an off-shoot of the work, that you begin to notice and observe more closely the actual movements and sounds carried out in real life by the characters in the situations you are portraying. Again, this should help you achieve the kinds of physical and vocal patterns which will achieve the effects you are aiming at.

By encouraging your child to listen, to watch and to copy you, you are developing his power of perception. By directing his attention towards the ordinary and familiar in an enjoyable play experience, you are helping him to take the interest in the world around him that he needs to acquire in order to develop his imagination and curiosity. By closely observing his reactions to the work you should be able to assess whether, and in what directions, he appears to be making progress. This, in turn, will help you to plan lessons which will emphasize and reinforce these areas, thus increasing the chance that your child will continue to make progress.

As he becomes more imaginative, more curious and more adept in the acting out process, there will be less need for you to demonstrate what is required. At this stage in the work, and with older, more able children, your role will be to make suggestions which will extend his range of play behaviours, provide a number of possible ideas from which he can choose in developing a particular play sequence, and help him organise his imaginative play by taking a supporting role and interacting with him in the situations he chooses to act out.

WHAT PROBLEMS CAN OCCUR?

In very many cases, the drama work you carry out with your child will be relatively straightforward to present and the experience will be an enjoyable one for both you and your child. In any teaching situation, however, there will inevitably be occasions when the work goes less well and when problems occur which make it more difficult for the child to master what he is being taught. Sometimes, all that is required is a reappraisal of the situation. Have you tried to progress too quickly? Have you been using the same material for too long, or for too short a time to make an impact? Is the material too easy, or too difficult? Is there a need to bring a new element into the work by introducing other people, or by asking someone else to take over for a time in order to provide variety in the presentation? Answering these questions will probably involve a process of observation and of trial and error, in which you try out new approaches or material and note whether this, in fact, leads to an improvement in the kind of responses your child makes, or in his degree of enjoyment and absorption in the work.

There are, however, a number of other factors which can cause problems and, since these are related to the child's handicap, they may be less easy to deal with than simple problems which call for a change of material or approach. For example, I have already mentioned that one of the difficulties which can arise is that of the over-stimulation of a child who is naturally hyperactive, and I suggested that there could be a need to build into the lesson some form of regulating mechanism which would ensure that this does not occur. At the other end of the spectrum, there is the problem of the passive, lethargic child who appears to have little curiosity and who takes little active interest in his environment. Here you may need to know *why* the child is passive before attempting to deal with this. For

example, if your child is epileptic he may be on a high drug
schedule in order to control this, and you may well have
noticed that there are certain times of the day when he is
less responsive and alert than others. For such a child, the
extent to which you can catch and hold his attention and
get him to respond may very well depend on choosing the
time of day to carry out the work that coincides with his
periods of maximum alertness.

Some Down's children can also be very passive, and
recent research has suggested that these children need
more stimulation over a *longer* period in order to coax them
to action because they have a longer arousal and reaction
cycle than many other children. With some of these
children the answer may simply be to persevere in
presenting material regularly over a longer period of time
before they finally 'catch on' and begin to respond. With
others the way you present material may be crucial. You
may need to be even more exaggerated or bizarre in your
voice and movement patterns in order to provide a
stimulus which is strong enough to attract their attention.
Other useful ways of catching attention in this situation
are the introduction of unusual toys which make weird
noises, such as party squeakers, toy cars with police
sirens, a musical jack-in-the-box in which Jack appears on
the appropriate musical or verbal cue; or by producing
very brightly coloured or moving objects such as large
party balloons, a brightly wrapped parcel, a toy windmill,
etc. Once you have caught their attention by these means,
you can then introduce similar sounds or movements
made with your own voice and body to encourage your
child to copy you. By contrasting the real and the
imaginative elements in this way, you may succeed in
holding his attention long enough to get a response. The
good news for parents of such children is that research has
shown that, when you have once achieved a response by
these means, there is a strong possibility that you will be
able to repeat it, with similar results, on other occasions
and to use it as a basis for introducing new elements into

the work. Although such children take a long time to arouse, when you have succeeded in doing so they often remember what they have been taught for longer periods than is the case with children whose arousal and reaction times are shorter.

A similar procedure may be adopted with children who are passive as a result of poor hearing, poor eyesight, or general motor difficulties. Again, there is a need to provide an initial stimulus which is strong enough to attract attention and to follow this up with movement and sound patterns which are large and clear enough to be obvious even to children whose physical problems make perception difficult.

Finally, there are children who are passive because of autism or severe emotional disturbance. Here it is very difficult to predict how they will respond to drama work. Some respond very quickly and easily, and seem to find in the work a means of expression which, because it is based on 'pretence', may be less difficult for them than the ordinary forms of expression open to them in daily interactions with others in real situations. On the other hand, if you find that your emotionally disturbed or autistic child appears to react with agitation or increased disturbance when you try drama with him, (and, although this is rare, it can happen), do *not* persevere with the work. It may be that, for your child, it is necessary to provide a more therapeutic form of drama than that suggested in the activities in this book, and this is really the province of the specialist drama-therapist or the psychologist. If, however, there is simply *no apparent response*, it might be worth while to persevere for a little longer to see what happens. Sometimes there is a continued lack of response. This can be a frustrating, discouraging and demotivating experience for you and you may feel tempted to discontinue the work. If, in spite of feeling this way, you can continue to persevere – even if you do so at less regular intervals – you may find that the continued stimulation you are providing does, in the long term, produce a response. In these circumstances you sometimes find that your child has absorbed more of what you were teaching than was apparent from his earlier behaviour.

A child who has a tendency to be aggressive or destructive may, paradoxically, present fewer problems in individual drama work than in many other situations, because the work itself can provide him with an opportunity to work off his aggressive or destructive energies in forceful patterns of sound or movement. I have found that such children rarely display real aggression in the course of individual work, although this is not necessarily the case when the child is working as part of a group. For such children, individual work carried out with a supportive adult, can go some way towards providing them with the stimulation they need, without placing them in a social situation which involves other people and makes undue demands on their capacity for peaceful co-existence. It also gives them the opportunity to gain approval rather than censure for their behaviour by being praised for the energy they can display in active pretence. Sometimes this can lead to better social behaviour in other situations, but this is not always so. Nevertheless, the drama session may be a time when parents can achieve a rapport with their difficult child and establish some form of pleasurable communication with him.

To sum up, therefore, the most common problems which can crop up in drama work arise out of individual personality traits in particular children. As a parent you are likely to know, better than anyone, the particular traits of your own child. Knowing this, you will be in a good position to judge the extent of the stimulation he may need, the ways in which his behaviour may need to be controlled and the kind of rewards to which he will respond. What I have tried to do in this chapter is to suggest some general ways of meeting difficulties when, and if, they arise. I should, however, like to end the chapter on a more optimistic note and emphasize the fact that, although problems can and do occur from time to time, for the majority of children, and, on most occasions, drama will be a pleasurable activity which parents should be able to tackle using their existing skills, experience and knowledge of their own child.

5   The Role of the Teacher

In the last chapter I suggested a number of ways in which parents could introduce drama to their younger children, and could provide regular opportunities for drama which would supplement the work done by the teacher, at school, with older children. I suggested that this work could be carried out on an individual basis, with parents working in a one-to-one relationship with their own children. Within schools, however, there may also be a number of children who need individual help and attention from the teacher in a one-to-one relationship. But, whereas parents may be working to provide *additional* help for their children by individual instruction, teachers are likely only to work on a one-to-one basis with those children who are not yet ready for group work and for whom such individual instruction is a *necessity*. Two types of children will need this help. The first are those children who are so behaviourally disturbed that they find it difficult to work within a group situation, and who make group work difficult for others. The drama activities and techniques which teachers may employ in working with such children are likely to be very similar to those described in the previous chapter. The problems encountered, and the ways of dealing with them, are also likely to be similar. In this situation, the teacher, like a parent, can concentrate on providing instruction which is geared exclusively to the needs of the individual child. Because social pressures are reduced, behavioural problems may be correspondingly reduced and the difficult child may be more amenable to instruction and learning under these conditions.

The other type of child who will need individual instruction is the child who is at a very early developmental stage, regardless of his chronological age. In the early stages of working with such children, much of the work may need to be based on a process of trial and error, in which the teacher experiments with a number of different activities in order to discover those which appear to achieve a response. This response will determine the direction of future work and give the teacher an indication of how she should proceed. At this stage, the teacher's aim will be to provide the child with strong sensory stimulation in order to attract his attention, to sharpen his perceptions and to arouse and motivate him to respond. In effect, she is feeding in information which should help the child learn how to imitate. Thus, at first, the child simply copies the teacher's behaviour – her sounds, her vocalisations, her movements, etc. Only when this imitation has been established will the child be able to engage in the kind of deferred imitation involved in 'pretence'. Therefore, although teachers may be using early drama activities with such children, these are being used less as an experience of imaginative, dramatic play than as a means of providing additional stimuli which will motivate the child to perceive, attend to and, eventually, make sense out of the sounds and movements occurring in his environment.

With some children, at this developmental stage, drama activities may not get any response. If they do not, it could be that other forms of stimulus, or other teaching strategies are more appropriate for that particular child. For those children who can respond, however such activities can provide an enjoyable basis for introducing new patterns of movement and sound. If a child can learn to enjoy making sounds and movements for their own sake, this should provide a means of motivating him to engage in the early forms of dramatic play as and when he becomes developmentally ready for these.

Fig. 1 gives an overview of the kinds of stimulus materia appropriate for use with children in these early stages, anc indicates possible directions for progressing with the work. Fig 2 gives an idea of the kinds of preparatory worl and teaching skills involved in the presentation of these activities. (Actual examples of these activities are not giver in this chapter, however, but are included in Part Two particularly in Chapters Seven and Eight.)

GROUP DRAMA

So far we have looked mainly at the ways in which the adult may introduce very early drama activities to childrer who need stimulation on an individual basis. But the majority of children in the six to eleven age-range are likely to be ready for group drama. For most teachers, therefore, the largest part of their work in drama is likely to centre on the provision of opportunities for children to work as part of a group. Since each of the children in the group wil have specific needs and individual interests, the teacher, in presenting group drama, has the additional task of balancing the needs of individual children within the group, and ensuring that all the children within the group have an equal opportunity to participate in the work. For example, the teacher may have to channel the energies of the more active or dominant group members, while, at the same time, trying to encourage the more withdrawn children to take an active part in the work. She will have to choose language, gesture or themes which can be understood by the less able children, while ensuring that these do not lead to boredom on the part of the more able children. In the course of the lesson, she will need to know how to build in opportunities for the children to contribute their own ideas to the work, how to accept these contributions and shape them into the progression of the lesson, and how to ensure that such freedom does not result in the lesson becoming chaotic and unproductive. Therefore to ensure that the work does progress, the teacher will need to know not only when, but how to

Fig. 1

EARLY DRAMA WORK

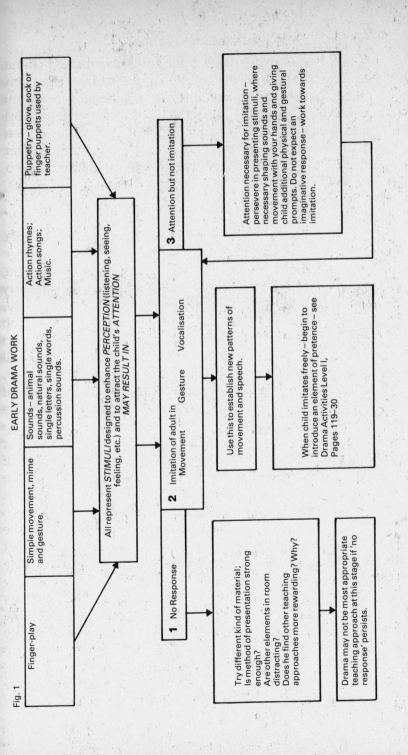

| Finger-play | Simple movement, mime and gesture. | Sounds – animal sounds, natural sounds, single letters, single words, percussion sounds. | Action rhymes; Action songs; Music. | Puppetry – glove, sock or finger puppets used by teacher. |

All represent *STIMULI* designed to enhance *PERCEPTION* (listening, seeing, feeling, etc.) and to attract the child's *ATTENTION MAY RESULT IN*

1 No Response

2 Imitation of adult in
Movement   Gesture   Vocalisation

3 Attention but not imitation

Try different kind of material; Is method of presentation strong enough? Are other elements in room distracting? Does he find other teaching approaches more rewarding? Why?

Drama may not be most appropriate teaching approach at this stage if 'no response' persists.

Use this to establish new patterns of movement and speech.

When child imitates freely – begin to introduce an element of pretence – see Drama Activities Level I, Pages 119–30

Attention necessary for imitation – persevere in presenting stimuli, where necessary shaping sounds and movement with your hands and giving child additional physical and gestural prompts. Do not expect an imaginative response – work towards imitation.

Fig. 2   PREPARATION AND TEACHING SKILLS

Finger-play; **Action rhymes;** **Action songs;** **Music**	*Preparation*– need to gather together a large repertoire of varied material (see Bibliography). Need to know material sufficiently well to use it without the aid of books, etc. which will hamper free movement. *Skills*– cultivate a flexible vocal range. Make use of dramatic pause, changes in rhythm, pitch and pace.
Movement sequences	*Preparation*– knowledge of range of difficulty in movement progressions – e.g. child may find it easier at first to copy movements such as touching his knees or feet which he can *see himself perform*, rather than movements such as touching his head or nose, which he can only feel. Knowledge of moulding techniques, guided imitation and shaping (again, see Bibliography for information on texts). *Skills*– ability to make clear unambiguous actions; ability to demonstrate movements and gestures in exaggerated form; willingness to make close physical contact with child in movement sequences.
Sound sequences	*Skills*– ability to make use of flexible vocal range described above; appreciation of association between sounds in the environment and vocal sounds; ability to combine sounds and movements in imaginative way.
Puppetry	*Preparation*– collect a large and varied assortment of puppets with different visual and tactile features (again, see Bibliography). *Skills*– ability to manipulate puppets in life-like way and to use sounds appropriate to the qualities of the particular puppet. Make physical contact with the child through the material of the puppet in order to provide variety of tactile stimulation.

intervene, in order to introduce new ideas or establish her authority in controlling the behaviour of individual children, without allowing the lesson to lose its spontaneity and enjoyment.

All of these are skills which teachers, experienced in teaching drama, will already possess. Inexperienced teachers may be less confident of their skills. But certain group drama activities are more situation-dependent than others and are consequently more demanding in terms of teaching ability. For example, in a lesson in which there is considerable freedom for children to experiment with responses and make a contribution, it may be very difficult to predict in advance how any particular group of children, or how any individual child within a group, will react in practice. If a teacher is reasonably confident of her inventiveness and her ability to 'think on her feet' she may well be prepared to tackle such a lesson, knowing that she will be able to accept and use virtually any contribution the children may make. On the other hand, a teacher who is less experienced, or less sure of her skill, may prefer to use activities in which the progression of the lesson can be fairly tightly structured in advance. This makes it difficult to lay down any hard and fast rules as to the particular emphasis which an individual teacher may need to place on control, on intervention, or on allowing children freedom to experiment in any given situation.

Fortunately, discussing the theory and principles of teaching drama is, in my experience, more difficult than actually doing drama with a group of children. When faced with the hypothetical question – 'what would you do if . . .' it is possible to take time to decide on what appears, theoretically, to be the best course of action. In the process, a number of different problems and solutions can be examined. But, when faced with a group of active, vocal children the question is more immediate. 'What do I do now?'

What you do will depend, not only on your skill, experience and knowledge of drama, but it will also depend, to some extent, on your own personality, and on the kind of drama activity that suits your own personal teaching style. For example, teachers who find it easy to adopt and maintain a role may prefer to work on improvised drama in which the teacher takes a role within the drama. In this way teachers can establish control, authority or progression as part of the drama being enacted. Teachers who are less happy to work in this way, and who prefer to remain in their role as teacher, may need to choose different types of material, such as narrative dramatisation, and to structure the lessons around a previously determined sequence of events. With practice and experience, of course, these preferences may change.

Nevertheless, just as in individual work there will be a period of trial and error in which the teacher feeds in different kinds of stimuli in order to discover which gets a response, so, in group drama, there will be a period at the start of the work in which the teacher is trying out different kinds of activities in order to determine which seems best suited to the capabilities of the group and, equally important, which she herself feels confident of tackling on a more regular basis. I believe, very strongly, that there is no single 'right' way to teach drama. Because the teacher herself is such an important resource in any drama lesson, the 'rightness' of any approach will be determined by how useful it is to a particular teacher's purposes, and by how well it fits her personality and teaching style.

Simply to say that there is no 'right' way to teach drama, however, is not particularly helpful to the inexperienced teacher who wants to know how to begin, the kind of material to use, and the techniques which may be available to her. So, before looking at some practical examples of drama in action, it might be useful to provide an indication of the kinds of teaching skills required in presenting different types of drama, and to look at the degree of difficulty which various activities hold for children. Teachers may then judge for themselves which of these activities seem best suited to their existing skills. By starting with those activities which you feel reasonably confident of tackling, you will gradually acquire, in practice, the more situation-dependent skills which we will look at in more detail in the practical examples given in the last part of this chapter.

GROUP DRAMA ACTIVITIES
The activities which are most commonly associated with group drama are:

Dramatic Play
Role Play
Improvisation
Dramatisation
Mime and movement
Speech activities
Puppetry

In addition, there are a number of activities, such as using music and especially percussion instruments, which can act as a stimulus, as sound effects for lessons, or as an integral part of certain movement and speech activities.

Dramatic Play/Role-Play/Improvisation
In chapter 1 we looked at spontaneous dramatic play and at what it entails. This form of spontaneous dramatic activity is considerably less demanding than the dramatic play which occurs within the group drama lesson. In spontaneous dramatic play the child is free to adopt or discard a role at will and the play does not require to be structured towards any specific purpose. In dramatic play within the drama lesson the child has to learn to interact and to co-operate with others in the course of his play, and to act out situations which have been suggested to him by another person.

Some theorists do not make a distinction between dramatic play, role play and improvisation, preferring to see them all as imagined situations in which a child acts out a role. Others suggest that dramatic play is the acting out of events and situations, while role play is more concerned with acting as a particular character and engaging in the kinds of situations which are appropriate to that character and the way he feels. Improvisation is an amalgam of dramatic play and role play, and, in improvisation, there is more emphasis on the use of dialogue. Since each of these situations calls for slightly different skills on the part of the pupils and teacher, I prefer to make a distinction between them.

Thus, dramatic play might involve, for example, acting out the events which occur when a car sticks in the mud. The roles adopted in relation to the car are only important in that different characters may react in different ways to the same situation. The emphasis, however, would be on what the characters did, and what happened as a result. In role-playing the emphasis would, in the same situation, be placed on the way the characters related to each other and to the event. Were they upset? Why? Why was it important to get the car out of the mud? What would happen to the characters if they could not get the car out, etc.? In an improvisation based on the same situation, what the characters said to each other would be just as important as what they did and how they felt.

Less able children may find it easier to suggest 'what to do' than say 'how it feels' and, for this reason, such children may find situation-based dramatic play easier to carry out since it involves actions rather than words, and events rather than feelings.

In role-play the teacher needs to ask questions which will encourage the children to think about and make the kind of responses which are associated with the characters. For example, 'do you think the boy was happy? How did he show that he was happy? How do you think his big brother felt? Why would he be angry, etc.?' Having established how the characters felt, she then has to translate these feelings into action – 'what did the boy do to show how happy he was feeling? What would his big brother do, do you think?' In this situation the teacher needs to allow some time in the activity for them to discuss their feelings and this necessitates a degree of verbal ability on the part of the children. With children who are linguistically competent, and who enjoy using language, this may lead to a situation in which there is as much discussion as action. While both may be equally valuable, the teacher has to decide how much time she will allow for each in order to maintain a balance in the lesson between preparation and enactment.

Since children may be taking individual roles in the acting out, the teacher will have to ensure that the less verbal pupils are not left out, and that other group members remain involved even when they are not the central characters. This may mean that the teacher has to feed in extra information for the less able pupils in the course of the work. To ensure that all are working at roughly the same pace, she may also have to provide additional prompts for those children who complete their part in the activity more quickly. If individual children are left for some time with, apparently, nothing to do, there is a danger that they will either lose interest in the work or revert to some other, possibly disruptive, activity.

In dramatic play there will also be an element of discussion. But, in this situation the teacher's questions are more likely to be concerned with the events, and suggestions made by the children can be accepted and acted upon quickly. For example, in acting out the episode about the car, the teacher might say: 'So what did the boy do, then? He pushed the car? That's a good idea. Right everybody, let's push and see if we can move this car. Are you ready – Push.' In such a situation the suggestions given by the children need not be in words. Gestures may be equally acceptable. This allows the less verbal children to participate fully in making a contribution to the work. Since less time is taken up in discussion, and since the actions suggested can often be performed by the whole group at the same time, the sequence of events is easier for the teacher to manage. If the teacher can join in with the actions, in role, she is providing a guide as to what to do, when to start, when to stop, etc., without having to stop the dramatic action for explanation or direction. This 'talking through' by the teacher in role can be very helpful to those children who find it difficult to know what to do next and can provide a check on the exuberance of the more active children. As children become more practised in drama work, the teacher may have to use this process of 'talking them through the events' on fewer occasions.

Thus, for children who are less able to use language and who need a degree of direction in knowing how to respond, dramatic play may be less demanding, and more within their capabilities, than role play. For the teacher, too, dramatic play may be less demanding in that it may create fewer opportunities for children to be uninvolved and, potentially, difficult to control. Children do, however, need to be able to work as part of a group – often in close physical proximity. Occasionally this physical closeness can trigger aggressive behaviour in potentially aggressive children. If the teacher knows that there is such a child within the group, she would be wise to stay fairly close to him throughout the work and, if she does adopt a role, to ensure that this role is one which will allow her to take control if there is any sign of aggression. It goes without saying that in any drama work in which the teacher adopts a role, she needs to be convincing.

In adopting a role within the less tightly structured role-play situation, the teacher will have to keep a part of her attention on what individual children are doing, and to be able to think quickly enough to involve all of the children by what she does or says in role. Role-play, then, is more demanding on pupils and teacher. Nevertheless, for pupils who have fairly good ability to use and understand language, it is a useful means of exploring 'real' characters and issues rather than the more stereotyped characters which may emerge in dramatic play. It also provides more of a challenge, forcing the children to think out what is involved in a situation and express the character's feelings in words.

Improvisation is more demanding on pupils than either role play or dramatic play. There is a greater emphasis on the use of language, not only in discussion but as part of the dramatic action. What is said in the acting out is just as important as the action, because this helps establish how the characters feel about themselves, about each other, and about the situation they are involved in. Before pupils can become fully involved in improvisation, therefore, they need a degree of fluency in speech, and the ability to interact verbally with either the teacher or other group members. Again, discussion determines what happens next and why. However, in acting out, pupils may not always follow the agreed course of action. If one child introduces a novel element, and if the other children react appropriately to it, this may change the whole direction of the work. This is to be welcomed as a sign that children are thinking for themselves. On the other hand, it is in this situation that the teacher needs to be confident of her ability to take control and direct the activity, if and when this appears to be necessary – either to keep the situation from getting stuck in a rut, or to prevent less able children from being put into an untenable position in the acting out. Again, if the teacher can adopt an 'authority role' within the improvisation – for example the captain of a ship, driver of a car, village leader, etc. – she may find it easier to direct and influence the course of the work without discouraging the children's contributions. Of the three, improvisation probably demands most sensitivity on the part of the teacher in knowing when and how to intervene, and greater acting ability in the adoption of a role within the work. The other skills required are very similar to those involved in dramatic play and role play.

Mime, Movement and Speech

The teaching skills involved in the presentation of such activities have already been discussed in relation to individual work. In group work, the approach adopted may be similar. Because everyone in the group is working at the same time on the same thing, there are fewer problems of pacing the work for the less able. The activity is directed almost entirely by the teacher, with the teacher providing a model for the children to copy, so there is less chance that the less able children will be left out, or that difficult children will be tempted to create disruption. The teacher can also feel reasonably secure that the way she has planned the sequence of events in the lesson is roughly how it will occur in practice. It is less usual for the teacher to take a different role from the children in this work. More often, she will be joining in with the pupils' activity, and providing a lead for this, as the teacher.

Such activities require a lower level of cognitive development than either role play, dramatic play or improvisation in that they are concerned with immediate imitative behaviour and appropriate responses. There is less need for children to think and plan what to do or how they feel. There will, therefore, be less discussion in such work, and, for most of the lesson, pupils will be actively engaged in the movement or speech activity being presented. Such work can be particularly useful for children who have poor verbal comprehension and expression, and who have poorly developed imaginations. It is for this reason that such activities were suggested as being more appropriate to children in the early stages of development. As the child matures, mime, movement and speech activities will tend to be subsumed within the more complex activities of dramatic play, role play and improvisation. More able children may find such teacher directed activities somewhat restricting in that there is less room for them to contribute their own ideas and actions. Opportunities can be built in for this, however, in even the simplest activity – children taking it in turns to be 'follow my leader', or to provide a movement or sound stimulus for others, being the obvious examples. Moreover, the very elements which can make such work restricting for such pupils are the ones which may help the less able pupils to become involved in the lesson. Children who have few ideas will be happy to follow the leadership of the teacher or the more able and, in the process, will achieve a degree of satisfaction. Incidentally, teacher-directed work of this kind is a useful lead in to drama work with children who have behavioural problems. The teacher can establish a degree of discipline in the work before risking the less tightly structured work involved in dramatic play or role play. The fact that she has established discipline in the lesson may make it easier for her to maintain this when she introduces these other activities.

Dramatisation

There are a number of different techniques that can be used in the dramatisation of stories and poems. These are given detailed consideration in Chapter 9. In the present context, it is sufficient to note that dramatisation can be taken at almost any level, from the simplest to the most demanding. At the simplest level the pupils will work as a group – all adopting the same character and carrying out similar actions in the story sequence. The teacher will talk them through the work in a similar way to that involved in dramatic play, but without necessarily adopting a role within the acting out. The most complex level of dramatisation is likely to be very similar to improvisation with the same level of skill being demanded of both pupils and teacher.

Basically, however, any form of dramatisation involves the same kind of sequence – choosing a suitable story or poem, selecting from that story the incidents one wishes to act out, and acting these out in an appropriate sequence. With non-handicapped pupils, or with the most able mentally handicapped pupils, the initial selection of the story may be made by the teacher, but the subsequent sequence may be largely in the control of the pupils, with some teacher guidance. With young, or seriously handicapped pupils, the selection and sequencing of events will be more teacher directed.

Children will need to have some comprehension of the verbally presented material before they are able to take pleasure in a storyline. Even for pupils with limited comprehension of verbally presented material, however, the changing facial expressions of the story-teller, the accompanying gestures and the changing vocal registers as she characterises the people in the story, may provide sufficient perceptual stimulation to catch their interest. This, in turn, may lead to an increased capacity for attention. Moreover, dramatisation has within it the possibility for introducing and experimenting with sounds. Children who have some difficulty in following the plot may nevertheless enjoy the sound and movement sequences in a story. Thus, when working with a group of very mixed ability, the dramatisation of a story may present an opportunity for work at various levels within the same activity, with the more able children appreciating and acting out the storyline with understanding, and with the less able children joining in the movements and sounds involved, without necessarily understanding the plot. As these less able children become more familiar with engaging in sound and movement sequences, however, they may gradually begin to realise the cause and effect involved in the story, and may begin to participate with more understanding.

While dramatisation that is developed round a pre-determined plot and character sequence may be somewhat restricting for the more able pupils, for the less able pupil the narrative outline can provide a framework within which he may develop his dramatic activity without the additional complexity of having to make up what happens next and to whom. Done in this way, dramatisation is a potentially less demanding activity than dramatic play, which is more open-ended. Moreover, some teachers prefer to work within a narrative framework in that this helps shape the progression of the lesson and much of what happens in the lesson can be planned in advance.

Puppetry

Puppetry, too, may be as sophisticated and demanding or as simple and undemanding as the needs and capabilities of the pupils dictate. The difficulties inherent in the more advanced forms of puppetry, such as marionettes, may make these too complex for the majority of seriously handicapped pupils. Even the effective use of a glove puppet can be fairly complex, involving, as it does, the close co-ordination of hands and voice. The manipulation of a rod or stick puppet, however, requires a much smaller degree of co-ordination, while the exaggerated features of papier maché puppets may stimulate the child to make a response, even if he cannot, himself, manipulate the puppet. Puppetry, therefore, can be useful as a stimulus to both individual and group work. It is also an activity which is suitable for children at virtually every developmental level. For the teacher, puppetry is one of the simplest drama activities to present in that, although children may be acting through the puppet, they will be less active than in any other form of drama work. For a teacher who is very unsure of her ability to tackle drama work in general, the use of rod or stick puppets, combined with a simple rhyme or action song, may provide a lead in. For the teacher who has a large number of multiply handicapped and wheelchair children in her group, puppetry may be an important part of the work as it can involve the least degree of physical movement of all drama activities.

SOME PRACTICAL EXAMPLES

These, then, are the main activities which are likely to be included within group drama work in the classroom. I have tried to show the different levels of difficulty involved in each, for both the teacher and the pupil, and to suggest the kind of skills required. As I said earlier, however, the particular approach adopted by an individual teacher will depend, to a large extent, on the kind of activity which she feels most confident of presenting. In the practical examples which follow I should like to share with you some of my own methods of intervention and control, and to examine some of the more situation-dependent aspects involved in the teaching of drama.

Example 1

The first example occurred during a lesson in which my aim was to encourage children to use the prepositions 'in/out/up/down' in appropriate ways. Over a period of several weeks we had done a number of movement and speech exercises involving the use of these words and we had gone on to a more imaginative situation in which the children, playing with a ball, repeatedly lost it and had to look up, down, in and out of various places in order to find it. As one of the group I tossed the ball and told the children that it had gone into the middle of a big puddle. The problem was how to get it out without getting our feet wet. We tried various manoeuvres without success, and I suggested that we would have to sit down and think of something else. At that point, George, one of the more able children in the group, stood up and began to mime something. I was not sure exactly what he was doing but, as he obviously had some idea, I suggested to the others that we should watch what he was going to do. Then I realised that he was miming removing his clothes. Within a few seconds he had plunged into the puddle and was 'swimming' out to get the ball. The 'swimming' involved a process of slithering along the floor, flailing his arms wildly. As soon as the other children saw what he was doing they began to copy him. A few obviously knew what was happening, but others were simply copying and enjoying the movements. Chaos reigned for a few minutes. Then George announced that he had found the ball and, holding it up, he waded back out of the water, followed by the others. We ran back home (to their desks) where we were able to change into warm dry clothing.

This example illustrates a number of points. First, it shows how the contribution of a single child can change the direction of the work. I had never envisaged that any of the children would think of swimming in the puddle. In fact, I had chosen a puddle in preference to a pool in order to avoid the possible chaos which might occur if they all went 'swimming' – especially since there were, in the group, a couple of very difficult, hyperactive children, who needed little encouragement to become over-excited in any movement-based drama work. Nevertheless they did all go swimming, and, although the activity became chaotic for a time, the chaos resolved itself without my having to intervene.

This raises the second point – when to intervene? If George had not found the ball when he did, I would almost certainly have had to find some way of ensuring that the more excitable children did not end up accidentally hurting themselves or someone else as they flailed around on the floor. In such a situation the temptation is to intervene as quickly as possible in order to make sure that order is restored and that the lesson progresses. But drama is, and should be, an active, vocal, social activity. Children are encouraged to move, speak and interact with each other and with the teacher. There is, therefore, every likelihood that there will be occasions when children become so involved in what they are doing that the general impression they create is one of chaos. I believe, however, that it is important to distinguish between the apparent chaos which occurs as a legitimate part of the lesson, and that which occurs as a result of children getting out of hand and behaving uncontrollably.

In this example George's actions were in keeping with the theme of the lesson. That other children would copy him was to be expected. Those who did understand the reasons for his actions were still involved in the imaginative theme of the play. Those who copied without understanding were not deliberately being 'difficult', but were simply enjoying the movement. Thus, while this particular episode was not an answer to the problem of how to get the ball without getting our feet wet, it was, nevertheless, in keeping with the problem, and presented a possible solution to it. If this episode had gone on for too long, however, it is doubtful whether the children would have been trying to solve the problem posed by the dramatic action. I suspect that, after a time, they would simply start to enjoy the movement, and when that point was reached, the movement work would be unlikely to contribute anything to the dramatic situation being enacted and the lesson would be unable to progress without some form of intervention.

However, such intervention can generally be accomplished within the general framework of the activity. For example, I might have said something to the effect of, 'Oh, look! There it is! I've found the ball. Can you help me push it out to the side of the puddle?' If one or two individual children had not accepted this verbal prompt, I might have taken them by the hand and said something like, 'Alan, Jane – look. The ball's down there, see? Can you help me?' Generally speaking, a gentle physical or verbal prompt of this kind is all that is required to ensure that the lesson moves forward. If, however, such a prompt had proved ineffective, it might have been necessary to take a more controlling role and offer an alternative opinion. For example, I might have said, 'Here's the park-keeper coming. Quick, out of the puddle before he sees you. Come on. Run back home as quickly as you can.' This distraction ought to be enough to ensure that the children are once more attending to the teacher and looking to her for what comes next. In this way the teacher can again assume authority without being too overtly authoritarian.

I am not suggesting, however, that the teacher should have total control of the lesson. Nor am I suggesting that freedom and spontaneity have no part in the lesson. What I am advocating is that the teacher tries to find ways of ensuring that, within the lesson, there is a balance of freedom and discipline. And I believe that this balance is important, for two reasons. First, because in any lesson or series of lessons, there will be some definite aim in view.

This aim might be as specific as the one mentioned in the above example, or it might be more general – for example, encouraging co-operation or imagination. Whatever the aim, however, the lessons will have been planned and the material chosen and presented in such a way that the children should gain the specific experience that will help them achieve the learning aim of that particular lesson. If the lesson disintegrates into a chaotic – but possibly highly enjoyable – free-for-all, it may be difficult to achieve the planned aims. The children may simply use up physical energy and enjoy themselves without learning anything very much, or they may develop a stereotyped pattern of repeating the same kinds of activity in the same way on each occasion. Thus the more able children are not being 'stretched', while the less able may find the whole experience a bit intimidating and opt out of participating in it. In order to achieve the aims of lessons, and in order to cater for the needs of individual children within the group, therefore, the teacher has to exert some control within the lesson. Secondly, and equally important, a situation in which children are out of control, and are not learning, can be a frustrating experience for the teacher. This, in turn may reduce the amount of pleasure she gets from the lesson and may, eventually, lead to her avoiding drama. And this would be a pity when one considers how much children can benefit from lessons which are planned and progress fairly smoothly.

On the other hand, if the lesson is so rigidly structured that children cannot make any spontaneous contribution to the work, the aims of the lesson may be achieved but at the expense of allowing the children to develop their own ability to take some responsibility for their conduct and decisions. So the rules I have made for myself are these:

a   Even within fairly tightly structured lessons, try to build in some opportunity for children to contribute.

b   If children are not ready to make a contribution – either because they have insufficiently developed imaginations or because they lack the self-discipline to do so without becoming disruptive – continue with the lesson as planned, feeding in the information necessary for the lesson to progress.

c   If the contribution that the children make is in keeping with the dramatic action, accept and use it.

d   Do not intervene too soon – sometimes an action which appears inappropriate can, if you wait and see how it develops, prove to be appropriate after all.

e   In cases of aggression or disruption – i.e. if the child's behaviour is *obviously* inappropriate to the dramatic situation – intervene quickly, in role if possible, in order to prevent problems.

f   If, as a result of the contribution made by one child or group of children, the direction of the work changes and control of the lesson passes to the children, allow them to exercise this for as long as the work progresses in an appropriate direction, and providing it does not leave less able children uninvolved.

g   When intervention does appear to be necessary, exercise the minimal control necessary to establish direction or progression; increase the degree of 'authority' only if it becomes necessary and attempt to do so within the context of the dramatic action whenever possible.

As you will see from these rules, I prefer to work within a fairly disciplined situation. I like to be sure that I can maintain, or regain, control of the lesson whenever I feel it is necessary, and I prefer to work in role if possible. Other teachers, with different personalities or approaches to the teaching of drama, may adopt quite different strategies. Therefore the precise strategies adopted are, I believe, less important than the fact that a teacher has learned to identify, for herself, the situations which she feels happiest with. So, rather than try to provide any more 'hints and tips' I should like to end this chapter by providing three more examples of situations which I have encountered and to pose a number of questions about these. The way each teacher answers these questions may help her identify the approach best suited to her own teaching style.

Incidentally, these are the types of questions which, applied after a lesson in drama, may help you assess how the lesson has gone. Assessment of what pupils have learned is likely to be achieved by observation of their behaviour both within and after lessons, and by noting whether there is an increase in the particular elements aimed at within the lesson.

Example 2

In a lesson designed to encourage children to differentiate between 'noisy' and 'quiet' and to use these qualities in speech and action, children were acting out a dramatic play situation involving Mr Noisy and Mr Quiet. All the children were taking both roles alternately. With one child, Mr Noisy was rather more popular than Mr Quiet. When all the other children in the group were being Mr Quiet, he persisted in being Mr Noisy. This did not appear to affect the other children, who ignored him and continued to be Mr Quiet.

Questions

a   Would you feel a need to intervene in this situation?
b   If not, why not?
c   If so, why? How would you intervene?
d   Could this situation have been avoided? Why, or why not?
e   To what extent could this situation prevent you from achieving the aims of the lesson with some/all of the pupils?

Example 3

In an improvisation designed to stimulate imagination, the children were attending a banquet at the court of King

Neptune. In the course of the banquet a cabaret was performed. It included 'the fighting swordfish', 'the dance of the eels', and 'the octopus band'. When it was time for the octopus band to play for the King, one non-verbal child came and took me by the hand and tried to pull me to the door. Katy was a child who had a number of unexplained fears and phobias, and her behaviour was often bizarre and unpredictable. I questioned her to find out what she wanted, but she became very excited, pulling and pushing me forcibly towards the door.

Questions
a   What would you think/feel in this situation?
b   What would you do? Why?
c   How would you cope with the insistence of the child?
d   What about the other children?

What I did, in fact, was suggest to the others that Katy seemed to want me to go away. Katy shook her head at this suggestion. I went to the door with her and opened it. When we were in the corridor she darted down it and into the hall. My reaction was that something in the lesson must have upset her. But I was undecided what to do. I did not want to leave the other children unsupervised but, obviously, did not want to leave Katy in the hall unattended. I leave you to draw your own conclusion on this one:

Questions
a   What would you have felt?
b   What would you have done?
c   Could this situation have been prevented? Why, or why not?
d   Should this situation have been prevented? Why, or why not?

Let me tell you how it resolved itself. Katy returned

within a few minutes carrying a guitar which was kept in the hall. It transpired that she had decided she wanted to play the guitar in the octopus band!

Example 4

The activity was dramatic play. The aim – to encourage children to co-operate with each other in a shared activity. For a few days prior to the lesson there had been some heavy falls of snow in the district. I decided to capitalise on this and to base the lesson on building snowmen, etc. I introduced the activity with a rhyme about a snowman. Then we 'dressed' in hats, scarves, boots, etc., and went 'out' into the snow, where we had a snowfight. Two children, Paul, and his friend Alan, had taken little interest in the activity up to this point, although all the other children had entered into it with gusto. Paul was a fairly intelligent child with good speech. Alan was less able, but tended to copy Paul. Paul said that he was going to make his own snowman. He took a box containing polystyrene chips and began to build a snowman in the box, providing a running commentary on his actions as he did so. Alan immediately copied him, and the other children said they wanted to build their own snowmen too. I agreed, and each child took a different article – a box of bricks, the sand tray, etc., and began to build. As they did so, I walked round and asked each child to tell me about his snowman. This took some time, and, by the end of the lesson we had a very strange collection of snowmen. At my suggestion, the lesson ended with all of us, including Paul, walking round, looking at each of the snowmen in turn and saying the rhyme which had introduced the activity.

Questions

a   Note the aims of this activity – to what extent were they achieved?

b   Was any other learning achieved?

c   How would you have handled this situation?

d   Would you have regarded this as a successful or unsuccessful lesson? Why?

6 Starting Off and Developing a Theme

In the last chapter I mentioned the possibility that, in introducing either group or individual drama work, there will be an initial period during which a variety of single lessons and approaches are tried out in order to establish those which appear best suited to the capabilities of the pupils and the teaching styles of the adults concerned. I have also stressed the fact that a regular and systematic programme of instruction in drama is likely to be necessary if maximum benefit is to be obtained from the work. But, whereas the single, trial lesson may be relatively easy to devise and plan, the planning of a regular programme of systematic work may be more difficult. First, a series of lessons obviously needs more material. Secondly, this material needs to be organised in such a way that earlier lessons lay the foundation for the gradual introduction of more complex ideas and activities. It is necessary, therefore, to look at the whole series of lessons in the planning stage in order to determine what needs to be taught first, the sequence of activities, and the kind of material which will allow new learning to be introduced at a later stage.

This can be a time-consuming task, especially for the general class teacher and the parent, both of whom will have many calls on their time other than the planning of a programme in drama. Even for the specialist drama teacher, who sees a great many different classes in the course of the week, the time pressures involved in finding material and in planning activities can be considerable.

Over the years, therefore, the method which I have adopted in coping with these pressures is that of basing lessons on a thematic approach. This approach is one which is neither new nor unusual. Teachers in all subject areas have been using it for years. And perhaps this, in itself, attests to its usefulness. To me, its value lies in the fact that one theme can generate a great many ideas, and can very easily be linked into and form the basis of a new theme, thereby giving an overall structure and progression to the work. This is more difficult to achieve if topics are introduced randomly and with no real relationship between them.

Within virtually any theme there is the possibility of working at almost any level from the simplest to the most advanced. This means that you can return to the same themes and explore them in more depth as the children mature and develop. It also makes it easier to plan lessons which are related to topics which have been introduced by other methods in other areas of the curriculum. So, before going on to the activities which make up the practical section of this book, I thought it might be useful to show how a series of lessons may be built up around a very simple theme with which even the most seriously handicapped child is likely to be familiar.

Familiarity is important since what tends to catch, and hold, our attention, as human beings, is a mixture of the familiar and unfamiliar. For example, most people, overhearing their own name in a crowded shop or restaurant, would automatically respond, and the natural reaction would be to look round to see if they were the subject of the conversation. If the speaker were totally unfamiliar they might naturally conclude that the conversation did not concern them, would lose interest in it, and would quickly cease to pay any attention to it. If, however, the speaker's face were vaguely familiar, it might well take longer for them to decide whether or not to go on listening, and, even after they had decided that the conversation did not concern them, they might well continue to puzzle over where they had seen the person before.

Psychologists and educationalists have recognised that this aspect of human behaviour is a potentially valuable one for teaching purposes, and they have suggested how to make use of it by advocating that new information be presented within the context of the familiar, thereby making it more likely that the attention span will be lengthened sufficiently for the new learning to take root. This new learning, in turn, becomes familiar and can, itself, form the basis for additional learning. And so the learning cycle progresses – each new item of information following naturally from the one before and paving the way for the next. So in developing a series of lessons and in planning a theme it is a good idea to start with the familiar. In this case – a ball.

STARTING OFF
There can be few children who have not, at some point in their lives, played with a ball. Most children will be able to recognise a ball, and, even if they cannot yet say the word, will be able to understand what the word means. Introductory lessons, therefore, can be planned around movement work based on ball play – kicking, bouncing, rolling, throwing, etc. All are natural movements with which children are already familiar and of which they have already had experience using a real ball. The plans for the first few lessons might look something like this:

Aims   To establish that children can carry out, on request, the simple natural movements involved in miming ball play.

Introduction
Explanation that the adult has a 'pretend' ball. Demonstration of how to throw and catch it. Give a pretend ball to each child. Ask the children to hold up their balls and say what colour the ball is that they are holding.

(This helps establish the reality of the pretend object for each individual child. The child who cannot think of a colour, or who does not yet fully understand the pretence element is, nevertheless, likely to participate by copying the words and actions of other pupils and/or the teacher.)

Activity

1 *Whole group:* throw the ball in air and catch it, varying the height of the throw.

2 *Whole Group:* take it in turns to throw the ball to the teacher, who catches it and throws it back.

3 *In pairs:* throw a ball to each other.

4 *Whole Group:* kicking and 'dribbling' with ball.

5 *Whole Group:* take it in turns to kick the ball at the teacher. The teacher may act as goalkeeper if the children are sufficiently advanced to understand this. If not, the teacher simply catches the ball, missing occasionally to give the children the satisfaction of beating her, and kicks it back.

6 *Whole Group:* bouncing the ball, and moving round the room while doing so.

7 *In Pairs:* 'heading' a ball to each other.

Final Activity (A calming and declimaxing period):
All the children throw their balls as high as they can; the wind catches them and they float away. Sit watching them float quietly away. Watch while the teacher's ball also floats up and away. Promise that they will be able to get the balls back to play with another day.

Depending on how well, or how quickly, the children have learned to cope with the pretence element in this activity, it may be necessary to repeat a very similar lesson on a number of occasions in order to establish what is required. When working with an individual child, rather than a group, the same sequence can be repeated, simply substituting 'child' for 'whole group'. This broad outline can form the basis of subsequent lessons in which one new element is introduced.

For example, an action rhyme may be added in one lesson to go with the movements:

> Throw the ball as high as you can,
> Up, up high!
> Catch the ball if you can –
> You can if you try!

Rhyme ✳

> or
>
> Bounce the ball, bounce the ball,
> One, two, three.
> Bounce the ball, bounce the ball,
> Throw the ball to me!

The words in these rhymes are sufficiently simple for some of the children to be able to join in after hearing them a few times. Even if they cannot yet join in with any of the words, however, the pairing of movement and rhyme helps to establish a co-ordinated rhythm in the movement work and helps them to respond fairly quickly to the movement commands contained in the words.

With a slightly more advanced group, it should be possible to combine the various kicking, heading and catching movements in a football sequence in pairs – one child being goalkeeper, the other (or adult) a player. With a group of able children, it should be possible to create a football match, with the teacher as referee, and with the children as players and spectators. This may be linked with work on colour. Children can be taught to identify two colours and to name them, and these may be used as identification for each team. In art work, they could paint stripes of the colour for the appropriate teams.

In this type of football sequence some children, with a tendency to become over excited, can be detailed to join the teacher in refereeing the match. This keeps the child close to teacher, while giving him some responsibility within the activity. A more controlled movement sequence can be achieved if the match is played in slow motion, as an action replay. Any other sporting activity can also be done in this way. Since this is a fairly sophisticated concept, however, the group would need to be reasonably advanced in general ability, or to have had some previous practice in carrying out all the individual movements involved in a slow, controlled manner, before combining these into a sequence.

DEVELOPING THE THEME

Having established the miming of movements and activities with which the children are reasonably familiar, begin, over the next few lessons, to introduce different aspects of ball play. Mime the actions involved in golf, tennis or table tennis, and encourage the children to relate in movement terms to the different sizes, weights, and types of ball used in these. With some children it may be necessary to introduce these new aspects of ball play by allowing them to spend some time examining, playing with, and exploring the properties of the real objects, before asking them to imagine them and mime using them.

An intermediate step in this sequence, and one which helps to reinforce the properties of these different ball games, is to play a game in which children have to guess what kind of ball the adult is miming. When the children can do this, reverse the procedure and let the children mime while the adult, or other children, guess.

Having established this familiarity, a more imaginative sequence can be built up, involving, for example, a golfer who loses his ball in the grass/trees/water/sand, etc., and has to find it again before play can proceed.

DIVERSIFYING THE THEME

This type of activity leads on very naturally to dramatic play involving other types of balls which have been lost in other locations, and reinforces the somewhat abstract concept of cause and effect. Because the children acted in a particular way, the ball was lost. In order to find it, they have to take certain steps. This introduces an element of problem solving into the work. How, logically, do we go about the business of finding something which has been lost?

With a good group of children this could form a link into the more general concepts of 'lost and found', and could lead, for example, to dramatic play involving loss of money or a purse through carelessness, improvisation involving 'losing' as a result of accidentally breaking something, the making good of such a loss, the 'losing' of a pet animal either through its running away or through death (if the children can grasp this concept), role-play involving leaving an important parcel, an umbrella or some other item, on a bus or train, and, with older children, could lead on to an introduction to the work of the Police in respect to lost property, and the idea of a lost property office.

As you can see, we have moved a long way from the initial theme of a 'ball'. Nevertheless, this progression is a natural one, and one which allows the exploration of more complex issues within a context that has already become familiar. With less able children the progression will, naturally, be slower, and it may be in a different direction. Some time may have to be spent in establishing their capacity for pretence before introducing dramatic play sequences of this complexity. Thus, for example, having introduced movement work in which children pretended to *use* a variety of different kinds of balls, it might be necessary to move on to other movement work, possibly with a musical background as stimulus, in which the children themselves *become* the ball. In this case, the children would be encouraged to bounce, to curl up and roll, to jump in the air, etc. as if they were balls responding to the person using them. In this way the children are, very gradually, being introduced to the idea of pretending to be someone or something other than themselves.

Within one such lesson, it should be possible to

introduce the idea of an inflatable ball. Again, this may be demonstrated using the real object, and, subsequently the children can be encouraged to grow bigger (as the ball is blown up) and to become smaller (as the air escapes). Finally they collapse altogether.

This may be reinforced in a subsequent lesson in which the children mime blowing up a beach ball. In this case the sequence of activities could be:

1   blow up the ball (with strong 'wh' sounds);
2   it has a leak! ('sssssssss' sounds);
3   take it back to the shop to buy another, or take the new one provided by the teacher. (With verbal children this could involve simple dramatic play in which the children have to act out, or even mime, the return of the ball to the shop. With non-verbal children, or with children who have poor comprehension, the teacher may simply provide another ball. Children often find it fun if they have to have several balls before, finally, they find one which does not leak.)

With less able children the concepts of big and small may have to be reinforced by suggesting other things which can become big and small – balloons being a fairly obvious example. Other examples include candy floss which gets bigger as it is made, and smaller as it is eaten; plants or trees which grow up and are cut down; things which look as if they get smaller, but without really doing so – for example airplanes, cars in the distance; bubbles which get bigger and burst, etc.

With slightly more able children the concept of taking a ball back to the shop can lead into the idea of buying a ball – not for oneself, but as a gift for someone else. This can form the basis of a lesson in mime in which children try to wrap up the ball – which *doesn't* deflate! – for posting. The difficulties involved in securely wrapping a round object, can help introduce the differences between objects which have no flat sides and no corners, and those such as boxes or books, which are square or rectangular, and which do have these properties. This can link very simply with maths work involving circles and squares. It can also link with the idea of giving and receiving, as a lead into the giving and receiving of gifts at Christmas time, or as an introduction to the work of the postman who ensures that the gifts we send do get to the person for whom they were intended.

MORE IMAGINATIVE WORK
Children who have developed their imaginations through the kind of work described above, may be ready to enter into situations which are less tied to experiences that might happen in reality and which are based on more fanciful or adventurous ideas. For example, the idea of a 'magic' ball can be introduced at a variety of levels.

At the simplest level, the magic of the ball might simply be that it has the ability to change into different things. Initially, the teacher may suggest what the ball has changed into. Later, the children may be able to give ideas of what the ball has become. This enables children to gain experience of trying out different roles, or of learning how to act out a variety of simple imaginative situations using a variety of different objects. These objects may, initially, have a clear relationship with the ball i.e. they may all be round. For example, the ball may turn into a coin which may be used to purchase something; a goldfish bowl with fish in it which the children have to carry very carefully (and which they may be able to win as a result of throwing balls into empty bowls at the fair); a round box containing a hat – the children can become the person in the hat (a king or queen, a policeman, a bus driver, etc.) Or, and this is more likely if the children suggest the changes, the objects can be related only by the fact that the ball has changed into them, but may have no intrinsic relationship with each other. Alternately, the ball may proceed through a series of shape changes, for example the round ball becomes a square box containing biscuits or sticky toffees which the children can mime biting and chewing; this turns into a triangle, as in the percussion instrument which the children can mime playing in a band procession this becomes a wavy object such as a rope which can be jumped over or through, or a snake slithering through the grass, etc.

At the intermediate level, the magic ball could be one which, when approached, has the property of affecting the children's movement in some way. For example, they start off moving as themselves, but as they approach the magic ball they begin to move in a slow, controlled, robot-like way and finally come to a complete halt. Or the ball might make them move their limbs very fast, or in a very jerky fashion, or crawl, etc. This provides a simple, and relatively imaginative way of introducing a variety of movement patterns and encouraging them to move their limbs with more co-ordination and control.

With a more able group it may be possible to introduce a much stronger element of problem-solving into the work. In this case the magic ball contains a shiny key – the key to a box of treasure. But the children cannot approach the ball and get the key until they make up a suitable spell, or take some appropriate action which will get rid of the monster who guards the ball and the key. The adult becomes the monster, and the children have to decide what to do. The adult can, however, feed them appropriate information by saying, for example, 'Oh, I'm so tired. If only I had a pillow, I could go to sleep and forget all about guarding this ball. I wish someone would get me a pillow'; or, 'I hope they don't learn that the magic word is hocus pocus. If they say hocus pocus, I'll have to give them the ball'; or, 'Oh, I'm so hungry, I don't care about this ball. All I want is something to eat. Now if someone were to give me something to eat, I would give him the ball'; or, 'I *might* give him the ball'. The 'might' provides an opportunity to 'stretch' children and to get them to try out different ideas so that they really have to answer the challenge and solve the problem before they can succeed. It is also possible to extend the problem solving element into a subsequent lesson in which children, having succeeded in getting the ball, then have the problem of getting the key out of it. Is there an opening in it? Do they have to find another magic word? What would happen if they simply dropped it? Would it break? Would it just bounce? And so on. Incidentally, as in every improvisation sequence of this kind, the work is not only more advanced for pupils, but it is more demanding of the role-playing ability, quick thinking, and control of the adult.

A relatively simpler activity, but again one which is suitable for the more able child, is one in which the magic ball gets bigger and bigger until the children are able to step inside and go off to explore a strange new planet, or a kingdom under the sea. Because of the influence of television, a new planet in space, or an underwater world, may actually be an easier setting for the acting out of exploration than a jungle or desert, concepts with which they may be rather less familiar. In this situation the teacher can be the leader of the party and is therefore in a position to feed the information to them more obviously and directly.

All of the preceding examples have contained an element of the unreal or fantastic. Something which could not possibly happen in real life, but which, in the acting out, may teach something of the problem solving, or communication skills required in real life. Some children will not, however, have reached the stage at which they are capable of making the distinction between the possible and the impossible. For these children the work may be advanced by setting the dramatic activity within a situation which is real, but which is unlikely to be experienced by them. This can provide a more exciting context for the work for those children who are unable to move on to more imaginative themes.

Again, the work may begin with related ball play. Start by introducing the idea of juggling with balls. Lead on to juggling in pairs, to balancing a ball on the head, to balancing it on an arm, the nose, or trying to balance oneself on a ball. Eventually, over a number of lessons, these activities may be combined and the idea of a circus introduced – jugglers, clowns trying to balance on balls and being inept at it, seals balancing balls on their noses, acrobats who keep a ball turning in the air with their feet, walking the tightrope while rolling a ball along one arm, down their chest, and along the other arm, etc. Again, all of these may be practised separately before combining them into a sequence as a circus.

This may sound like a very complex activity for children to cope with. And yet, when it is analysed, it can be seen that it is based on the relatively simple movements and concepts which were established in earlier lessons – throwing and catching, bouncing a ball, being a ball, heading a ball, using the feet to control a ball in kicking, or while running, and taking on different roles in relation to a ball. The complexity of the less familiar elements – seals, tightrope, acrobats – can be reduced, if only one new element is added at a time. To get to the point at which the children are ready to act out something as complex as a circus, therefore, may involve something like a whole term's work. But, although the final dramatic sequence achieved may be complex, each individual lesson in the series ought to be relatively easy since the skills introduced in one lesson are being practised, reinforced and expanded in the next. And, when they are analysed, it will be seen that most complex activities can be broken down in this way into reasonable simple sequences which can be taught in progressive stages over a period of time.

Thus, the aim of the first lesson in this theme – to establish mime based on the natural and familiar elements of ball-play – has gradually been replaced by other, more complex aims such as establishing the ability to imagine and act out a role, encouraging a more flexible range of body movements and more co-ordination in movement, expanding the vocabulary to introduce new words and phrases, linking with work on maths or colour naming, problem solving, and so on. From the simple and familiar theme of a ball, therefore, it is possible to plan a whole series of learning experiences which can range from the simplest movement and speech activities to considerably more advanced work involving co-operation, problem solving, and the introduction of abstract concepts such as large/small, lost/found, square/round, etc.

Obviously, the rate at which you can progress, and the extent to which you can progress, will be governed by the individual capabilities of the children involved. Similarly, the particular direction in which you slant the work will be governed by such factors as the excitability and self-discipline of the children, their particular interests, the ratio of boys to girls, the space and time available to you in which to carry out the work, and the particular aspects of learning which are in keeping with your teaching aims. Nevertheless, I hope I have shown that adopting a thematic approach can make the planning of lessons which will take these factors into account a relatively simple task, and one which should avoid the common problem of knowing what to do next, and the kind of material to choose.

SOME FURTHER EXAMPLES

Before concluding this chapter, therefore, let me suggest a number of other possible ways of expanding this theme, all of which I have used at various times, with different groups of children and for different purposes.

Inflatable balls

1   With a group of young children who were about to go on a school trip to the seaside, the inflatable balls lesson provided a means of introducing the information and vocabulary which would prepare them for this experience. It led to a series of lessons involving the seaside – blowing up beach balls and playing with them on the beach;

blowing up a lilo and lying on it, splashing hands and feet in the sea; blowing up a rubber ring and going swimming; making sandcastles; attempting to put up a deckchair; buying an ice-cream, licking and eating it; travelling in a bus. These were eventually combined into a dramatic play sequence involving all the above, plus a heavy shower of rain which necessitated packing up everything, a quick dash for shelter, and the buying and eating of chips. Afterwards, they made a 'poem', which consisted of single words or sounds associated with the seaside, and they beat out the rhythm of the words on percussion instruments. This helped to reinforce the vocabulary, and, after the trip, the real events experienced were acted out as a means of consolidating both the vocabulary and the elements of the real experience.

2   Towards Christmas time, with another young group, consisting mainly of girls, the inflatable balls sequence provided a link with balloons, Christmas decorations, parties and carnivals. Although most children can enjoy playing with balloons, some can be afraid of the noise they make when they burst, and some children do not understand the excitement and noise generated by something like a Christmas party or carnival. The drama work provided a vicarious experience of these before the event. Practising the 'bang' a balloon makes when it bursts made this a more familiar and less threatening experience. The activities involved in decorating a room in preparation for Christmas, helped them understand the reasons for the changes in their environment at this time, and, again, helped lessen the fears which can occur when routine is disrupted.

3   With a slightly older group in which there was a high proportion of boys the inflatable balls sequence was diversified into a series of lessons which were geared towards the boys' interest in cars. This was approached

hrough the idea of other inflatable objects – car tyres, bicycle tyres, etc. This led on to work involving tyres which had punctures and which had to be repaired. This, in turn, led naturally into dramatic play involving buying petrol, the mechanical car wash, washing cars by hand, going for a trip in a car to have a picnic. A number of rhymes were introduced in the course of this work, and the work led on to the dramatisation of a story involving a car which had got stuck in the mud and which had to be towed out. The children were also encouraged to think about other kinds of cars and lorries. This work generated a great deal of conversation and helped create links with home, since the parents of all the children in the group had a car. As a corollary to the work, various collages were made out of photographs of cars, magazine cut-outs and the children's own art-work.

Parcelling a Ball

We have already seen how a lesson involving parcelling a ball can lead into either a series involving the abstract concepts of square and round, or the giving and receiving of gifts and the posting and delivering of parcels.

With a good group of children in which, again, there was a high proportion of boys, a number of whom were lively Down's Syndrome children who had poor speech, but a good range of gesture, the parcelling sequence led into a series of lessons involving other deliveries and services – milkmen; firemen; dustmen; window cleaners; etc. Because the children had poor speech, these activities were based on mime, but with the accompaniment of appropriate noises – for example the 'sh' of the fireman's hose; the 'clink' of the milk bottles; the 'crunch' of feet on gravel, etc. These were also linked to rhymes involving the sounds. In this way it was hoped that the children would have an opportunity to practise 'babbling', an important stage in the development of articulation, within an imaginative context which was in line with their chronological age and interests.

Jugglers

We have already seen how the throwing, catching, rolling and balancing of balls can lead to the theme of a circus. With a group of older, very passive girls, who needed to develop both their ability to move flexibly and their imagination, this led on to a consideration of other animals: zoo animals, domestic pets, farm animals. Having established some of the vocabulary and the properties associated with real animals, we went on to create 'weird' animals out of plasticene, pipe cleaners, and kitchen foil. We then worked on a series of movement lessons involving the strange movements of these weird animals, speech work involving the strange noises they might make when feeding, hunting, sleeping, etc. Eventually, we created a huge composite animal in which each child was a different part of the animal and was linked in some way to the next part. Working out how this animal would get from point A to point B without bits of itself becoming detached, proved not only a highly entertaining experience, but also provided a great deal of valuable discussion, and co-operative experimentation on what the animal looked like, which part would have to move first, how the various parts would move in unison or sequence, and the kind of sounds the animal would make as it moved. This was accompanied by electronic music which provided a stimulus for the weird movements of the strange animal.

In all of the examples given in this chapter, I have simply mentioned the kind of dramatic play, improvisation, or other material which could be used to support the theme. In the practical section which follows I have tried to suggest actual examples of material from which teachers and parents may select those activities which can be combined into a series of lessons of their own devising. In Chapter 11, however, I have included three graded examples of term-long thematic projects, including all of the materials used in these. I hope these will provide a useful model of how the general planning outlines indicated in this chapter can be translated into the practical business of starting off and developing a series of lessons in drama.

PART TWO

Speech and movement games, and
drama activities for use in small-
group and individual work

7   Pre-Drama and Early Dramatic Play Activities

All of the activities in this section are short, and most introduce only one central idea or theme. These activities are particularly useful for parents or teachers who intend to work on an individiual basis with young children, or with children in the very early stages of development of dramatic play. Teachers may also use some of the ideas suggested here with a small group as a lead in to more advanced work with children who have no previous experience of drama. Some of the ideas may also be adapted to suit children who are blind or partially sighted, or children who are physically handicapped and for whom mobility is a problem.

ACTIVITIES DESIGNED TO CREATE AN AWARENESS OF SOUND

In the games which follow, each game has been broken down into a number of progressive stages, and the games themselves are designed to provide a progression from the simple to the more difficult. Obviously, the rate at which you can proceed will depend very much on the ability of the individual child. With some children one stage of a game will constitute a lesson in itself, and each stage may have to be repeated several times before the child masters the game. This is perfectly natural for children in the early stages of development and should be no cause for concern. If, after five or six repetitions of the same stage, however, a child does not appear to master the idea, either change to a different game or go back one stage and consolidate it before moving forward again.

Game 1: What is Making the Sound I Hear?

This is a game designed to encourage the child to make an association between sounds and objects within a play situation. Children with poor sight may also take part in this game if they are allowed to feel the objects and, in this way, learn to make an association between them and their sounds.

You will need: a number of toys which are easily recognised by the child. If possible, choose at least one toy with which he is already familiar, and which has a natural association with sound, for example a toy cat – miaow (later, purr); a toy dog – woof (later bow-wow, yap); a toy duck – quack, quack; a toy clock – tick tock; an alarm clock – not a digital clock, but one with a tick and a bell.

Stage 1 Ensure that the child is seated and is attending to you. Choose one toy. Keep all the others out of sight for the time being. Hold up the toy, point to it, and say something like:

'Look, John! A clock. Listen to what the clock says.
Tick, tock, tick, tock, tick, tock. (Move clock from side to side)
Listen again. (Hold clock out to him)
Tick, tock, etc. (Move clock as before)
What is making the sound I hear?
Tick, tock, etc.
A clock is making the sound I hear! (Point delightedly to clock)
Tick, tock, etc.'

Repeat this a few times, exaggerating the pleasure you have in making the clock sound and in listening to it. Then go on to say something like:

'Can you make the clock go tick, tock, John?' (Let him hold the clock, but place your hands over his as he does so and help him to move it from side to side, as you say 'Tick, tock, etc.')

Again, repeat a few times till he gets the idea. Stop if he appears at all bored. Do not worry if he does not appear to understand or to respond at first. When he can join in with this stage of the game, move on to stage 2.

Stage 2   Introduce him to the toy again. Place it on the floor and say:

'We're going to play a game with the clock now, John. Can you show me what is making the sound I hear? (Quietly, getting louder) Tick, tock, etc.'

If he makes no move, take his hand and place it on the clock and say:

'Yes! A clock is making the sound I hear. It says tick, tock, etc.'

Note – the clock is *not*, in fact, making the sound. You are making the sound, and, if the child appears to recognise this fact and points to you, say:

'Yes. That's right, I'm making the sound of the clock. Tick tock. The clock says tick tock.'

This may seem to be making it more confusing for the child. However the aim is to encourage him to make the association with the verbal sound, the symbol, and the object which is associated with that sound, and to do so in a 'pretend' context. If you can establish this kind of association, the child is well on his way to understanding what it means to pretend. Therefore, go through it a few times, helping him to point to the clock and repeating the rhyme as a cue for him to point. If he manages to point correctly, unaided, show him how pleased you are, but do not show any disappointment if he fails to do so. When he can do so, go on to stage 3.

Stage 3   Repeat stages 1 and 2 several times, varying the toy used, for example:

> What is making the sound I hear?
> Miaow, miaow, miaow, miaow.
> A cat is making the sound I hear.
> Miaow, miaow, miaow, miaow.

At this stage, however, use only one toy per session. When he has succeeded in making an association with a few toys and their sounds, move on to stage 4.

Stage 4   Introduce two toys at the same time. Place them on the floor. Say the rhyme and see if he can guess which of the two toys is making the sound. Vary the sound of the toy and repeat, using the rhyme, until he can guess correctly. When he can do this using two toys, try introducing other toys, one at a time – in each case always one which he has already learned to associate with a particular sound – until he can guess correctly from a number of toys. When he can do this, move on to stage 5.

Stage 5   Choose one toy and give it to the child. Ask him to make the sound the toy makes. This may take some prompting, and may take a few sessions to establish. Praise him for any attempt he makes. When he can make any sound that is close to the sound introduced, even if it is only the 't' of tick, or 'a' for quack, for example, praise him and say:

> John is making the sound of the clock.
> Tick, tock, etc. (repeat)

Repeat this sequence with another toy. When he can make two sounds which are different for two toys, introduce a third. When he can make three sounds, go on to the final stage of this game.

Stage 6   This is the most difficult stage in this game, since you are attempting to get the child to make the sound of the object, purely on the basis of the name of the object, rather than by using his name in the rhyme. At this stage, explain that *you* are going to guess what is making the sound you hear. Let him choose one of two toys. Close your eyes and say, 'Now, what is making the sound I hear?' If he makes an appropriate sound, say, 'It's (pause), it's (pause) it's a clock. A clock is making the sound I hear.' Show him how delighted you are that you have been able to guess, and praise him. If he makes no sound, open your eyes and say something like:

> 'Oh, I didn't hear any sound. Come on, clock. Let me hear what sound you make. What sound does the clock make? Is it tick, tock? Yes. I'll close my eyes and guess again. What is making . . . etc.'

Eventually, the 'breakthrough' will come and, with it, the beginning of an understanding of what it means to imagine or pretend.

Game 2: Hunt the Musical Box
This game is no more difficult than Game 1 and may either precede or follow it. Again, the game has been broken down into a number of stages. The aim of this game is to encourage the child to learn that 'hidden' objects stay in the same place until they are found.

You will need: a musical box or other musical toy and a fine scarf.

Stage 1   Ensure the child is seated and attending. Show the child how the toy works and let him hear the music. Encourage him to listen to the music, placing the toy close to his ear, if necessary. (With some children one of the small musical toys, shaped like an animal and designed to hang on a pram, may arouse more interest than a musical box.) Once he shows that he can hear and enjoy the music, take the toy back and stop the music. Explain that you are going to hide the musical box and he has to find it. Start the music. Place the toy on the floor. Cover it with the scarf and make sure that he has seen you do so. Say:

'Where is it? Where is the musical box?'
If he tries to lift the scarf, praise him and say:
'Yes. there it is. Let's hide it again.' (Repeat sequence.)
If he does not try to lift the scarf, say:
'Now, I wonder where it is. Is it over here? (looking on floor to right.) No. Is it here? (looking on floor to left.) No. Is it here? (pause; lift scarf very slowly, bit by bit.) Yes! Here it is! We've found it.'

Repeat until he understands the principle of finding and hiding.

Stage 2   Vary the game by letting him hide the musical box and you find it. Gradually, introduce other hiding places which are a little further away, but still let him see where the toy has been hidden before he has to find it.

Stage 3   When he has become adept at finding a toy musical box which he has seen being hidden, get him to close or cover his eyes and hide the toy again. This time he has to find the toy on the basis of the sound alone. In effect, he is following the sound. At first, you may have to go with him and help him 'discover' it. As he becomes more skilled, it should be possible to take it in turns to hide and seek the music.

Game 3: Hunt the Dog/Cat/etc.
This game leads on from the two previous games and makes use of what the child has learned in these. The aim of this game is to encourage the child to respond to changes in the volume of speech. It is very similar to the party game 'hunt the thimble'. As with the two previous games, this game should also be possible for the child who

has poor eyesight; it is, however, less suitable for the child who has poor mobility.

You will need: the toys used in Game 1 and a fine scarf.

Method   Show the child one toy. Encourage him to make the appropriate sound with you. If he does not, you repeat the sound alone.

Stage 1   Place the toy on the floor. Make the sound fairly loudly, then cover the toy with the scarf and stop making the sound. Stop abruptly. Look surprised, and say:

  'It's stopped. Where is it? Where is the (name of toy)?'

Help him lift the scarf, and, as soon as the toy is revealed, start to make the sound again. Replace scarf and stop. Uncover, and start, etc. Essentially, all you are doing is playing the previous game, but, instead of using a toy which has a built-in sound, you and, hopefully, eventually your child will be making the appropriate sound.

Stage 2   When the child can either regulate your sound making by uncovering and covering the toy, or when he can make the sound at the appropriate time, dispense with the scarf. Instead, hold the toy in front of you and very gradually move it behind your back, making the sound more and more quietly as you do so, until the toy is out of sight. As you bring it back into view in front of you, increase the volume once more. Point out to your child that it gets quieter as it goes away and louder when it comes back. Repeat several times. Eventually, encourage the child to hold the toy, helping him if necessary, and encourage him to copy what you did in both sound and movement. With a blind, or partially sighted child, this stage, and the previous stages, will need to be talked through, and the child allowed to feel what you are doing so that the process is clear to him.

Stage 3 When the child can respond to the loud/soft sound by putting the toy behind/in front of him, and when he can make an appropriate level of sound for the actions as you do them, introduce the idea of the toy going away in other directions – up, to the side, etc. Make the appropriate level of sound as you do so. Encourage your child to copy you. When he can do so, let him control your volume by where he puts the toy. If he can also moderate his own volume on this basis, so much the better.

Stage 4 When the child can understand the principle – loud equals near, soft equals far – hide the toy further away. Let him see you hide it. Come back to him and together go and hunt for it with you making the appropriate volume of noise as you get nearer to the toy. Let him 'discover' it. When he can do this, with your help, encourage him to do it uinaided, but still let him see you hide the toy at this stage.

Stage 5 Hide the toy without his seeing where you hide it. Let him try to find it on the basis of your volume alone. A little physical help may be necessary at first, but eventually he should be able to find the toy on his own.

Stage 6 When he is adept at finding the toy on the basis of volume alone, reverse roles. Let him hide the toy and guide you to it on the basis of his volume alone. Most children find this a much more difficult task than any of the preceding stages, as there is little you can do to help, other than by saying something like:

> 'Ah. The noise of the clock is getting louder, so I must be near. What will happen if I go this way? Will it get louder? Or quieter?'

If the child does not moderate his volume when you give him such cues, confess that you are stuck and ask him to help you find the toy. Eventually, however, he ought to be able to guide you by making some change in the volume he uses, and, when he can do this, he is well on the way to understanding some of the elements which must be present before he can pretend: for example, the ability to link an object with a symbol which represents it, in this case a sound; the ability to understand that objects are permanent, even when they are out of sight; the ability to remember and recreate in imagination both an object and where it has been placed. In the process, the child should be learning to enjoy making sound as part of a pleasurable play experience.

Game 4: I hear with my little ear

This game is a sound version of the old favourite 'I spy'. This game consolidates the association between objects and sound, but the aim of this game is to encourage the child to make the association on the basis of memory and imagination alone – without having the objects physically in front of him. This is a more advanced game than any of the preceding, and it may have to be repeated a number of times to establish it.

Method   Explain that you are going to play a game in which he has to guess what you are thinking of. Use the same range of sounds introduced in previous games. Give him an example. Say, 'I am thinking of something that I can hear with my little ear and it sounds like this – miaow. It's a cat! I can hear with my little ear something that sounds like this – tick, tock. It's a (pause to see if he will answer) clock!' It may be necessary to feed the answers at first but, sooner or later, if he has been enjoying the games, the child should be able to guess unaided. When he can do so, let him make the sound for you to guess. Say:

'John can hear with his little ear something that sounds like... (If he doesn't respond right away try prompting.) What sound are you going to make, John? Are you going to make the cat sound? Miaow. Let me hear it? Miaow? Oh, good. Now, John can hear with his little ear something that sounds like a cat. Now you try again and I'll guess, etc.'

Eventually, the breakthrough should come and your child will be able to understand and play the game. On future car journeys, however, you may regret this. It is noisier than 'I spy' and, if your child has only a small range of sounds, can get monotonous. However, the range of sounds can be gradually extended by playing the games with a new range of sounds, and, eventually your child should be able not only to make the sounds but to label some of the toys as well.

Rhymes and Jingles
These are very simple. They make use of the same range of sounds already introduced, and provide a means of varying the lessons from time to time, by encouraging the child to make the sounds in a more rhythmic context. They also introduce the idea of big/little, which will be used in some of the movement activities which follow.

1 The big, big clock says TICK TOCK, TICK TOCK
   (*loudly, moving arms in broad arc from side to side*),
   But the little clock just says tick tick tick tick Tock.
   (*quickly and quietly, moving finger from side to side in time to rhythm, and ending on loud sound 'tock'.*)

2 In the morning, what do I hear?
   Brr, brr, brr, brr.
   The alarm is ringing in my ear.
   Brr, brr, brr, brr.

3 Here comes the big dog – BOW WOW WOW
   Here comes the little dog – yap, yap yap.
   Big dog! BOW WOW! Little dog! Yap, yap!
   What a row!

4 The man has a big drum – BOOM BOOM BOOM.
   The man has a little drum – tap, tap, tap.

BOOM tap, BOOM tap, BOOM BOOM BOOM.

5   Daddy duck says QUACK.
    Mummy duck says quack.
    Mummy duck and daddy duck say – quack, come back!
    And little ducks so far away,
    Bob their little tails and say
    Quack, quack, quack – we'll come back – QUACK.

6   I met a little pussy cat, the pussy said to me:
    Miaow, miaow, I'm hungry.
    I gave the pussy cat some milk, the pussy said to me:
    Purr, purr – I'm happy.

ACTIVITIES DESIGNED TO STIMULATE AWARENESS OF THE BODY

These activities can be taken either before or after the speech games, or, being of a similar level of difficulty, can be used alternately with the speech games to provide variety in the work.

Game 1: Big steps/little steps

This is probably the simplest type of movement activity. There is no imaginative content as such. What you are attempting to do at this stage is to encourage the gross motor skills involved in linking particular movements to a sound stimulus.

You will need: a small drum, beater and jingle bells, or other percussion instrument with a quick, jingly, sound.

Stage 1   At first, do not introduce movement. Show the child the instruments and how to operate them and spend some time establishing that he can enjoy making the sounds or listening to the sounds as you make them.

Stage 2   Use only the drum at this stage and show the child how you can take big steps in time to a slow, loud drumbeat, accompanied by the words 'big step'. Encourage him to make the drumbeat, giving him physical help if necessary, and try to get him to provide the beat for you as you do the actions and say the words. Later, take it in turns to beat the drum and to take the big steps.

Stage 3   Introduce the little steps in the same way but using the jingle bells to accompany the words. Introduce the command 'stop' and encourage him to stop on command. Praise him lavishly if he can not only stop but can stand quite still until the 'music' starts again.

Stage 4   Using both instruments, alternate big steps/little steps/stop – until the child can respond easily.

Stage 5   Using the drum, introduce jumping movements in the same way, but breaking up the word into two syllables – jump-ping – and giving a double beat on the drum. Other movements and their names may be introduced in the same way, but each new sound and movement should be introduced individually so that an association is built up between the two. When the child can understand and respond to a range of movement words, make a game out of varying the sounds and movements within one lesson, making sure that the drum beat or other instrument used is clearly differentiated for the different sounds and movements.

When the child has established a vocabulary of these large movements, he is ready to move on to action rhymes and games involving specific parts of the body, and using finer motor control.

Action Rhymes
1   This rhyme consolidates the movements already introduced.

> Look at me, look at me.
> I am hopping – one, two, three.
> One, two, three. Hop with me.
> We are hopping, one, two, three.

Vary the words to introduce other movements – we are running/rocking/jumping, etc.

2   Focussing on hands and feet:

> I have hands and I can clap them – clap, clap, clap
> John has hands and he can clap them – clap, clap, clap.
> I have feet and I can tap them – tap, tap, tap.
> John has feet and he can tap them – tap, tap, tap.

Demonstrate and give physical help if necessary. Incidentally, this rhyme is useful for children in wheelchairs, if the adult physically moves the child's limbs for him. Once this sequence has been established add new verses:

> I have hands and I can rub them/wave them, etc.
> I have knees and I can scrub them;
> I have toes and I can touch them/wiggle them;
> I have fingers and I can wiggle them, etc.

3   To the tune of 'There's a Worm at the Bottom of the Garden' make a game out of the words and movements introduced in the previous rhymes.

> I have feet at the bottom of my legs, and here's what my feet can do (repeat)
> They hop, hop, hop, hop all the day (repeat)
> I have feet at the bottom of my legs, do you have feet there too?

Make a game out of looking for the child's feet. With wheelchair children, restrict the movements mentioned to ones which the child can do. Encourage children to join in both the song and the actions, and vary the actions and body parts used – I have toes at the bottom of my feet; I have hands at the bottom of my arms; I have fingers at the bottom of my hands, etc. This can also make a good party game, especially if the children can understand and respond to the fun in words like wiggle/waggle/tip-toe, etc.

Game 2: Simon says

In the usual version of 'Simon Says' the words 'do this' signify that the actions have to be performed, while 'do that' is a negative command meaning, in fact, 'don't do that'. This confusion of commands would obviously be too difficult for many children. However, I find that a very simple version of the game is a popular and enjoyable means of reinforcing the making of physical movements on spoken commands.

You will need: a glove puppet who can be called Simon.

Method   Having introduced the puppet to the child, use the puppet to play the game. Instead of using the words 'do this, do that', simply introduce phrases: 'Simon says touch your toes/ Simon says clap your hands, etc.' The fun of the game is achieved by the variations in vocal pitch, pace and rhythm introduced by the adult. For example, a typical sequence might be something like this: 'Simon says (raising pitch of voice on says and elongating the word, pause) clap your hands (said quickly). Simon says touch your (pause) touch your (pause) toes. Simon says stand up/sit down/stand up/sit down (repeated quickly and ending with) Simon says stop.'

Game 3: Eyes close, touch your nose

This game is very similar to the previous one except that the puppet is not used and each command is prefaced by the words 'eyes close, touch your nose, eyes close touch your . . .' In this game, more difficult movements, involving actions which the child cannot see himself perform are introduced, for example touching the nose, the ears, the back, the top of the head, etc. These movements seem to be less difficult if the child has his eyes closed. I am not quite sure why this should be the case, but, in practice, it does happen.

Animal Movements

Having mastered a range of realistic human movements, the child is now ready to move on to more imaginative movements. Animal movements are particularly popular, and even children who have problems in relating to people often respond to movement and sound work which is based on animals.

In introducing these movements it is best to start with a related human movement which the child has already practised, for example:

hopping could lead to the movement of birds hopping and pecking at crusts of bread; crawling and stretching lead into cat movements, and these can lead into the movements of the larger cats – lions and tigers – with emphasis on the contrast between stillness and strength; running and jumping lead naturally to dog movements; etc.

EARLY DRAMATIC PLAY

In the earliest stages of dramatic play children need real objects around which to develop imaginative sequences. Dolls, soft toys and cars tend to be the objects most commonly used spontaneously by children. Many children will, however, need help in developing any form of dramatic play sequence with these or other toys. Helping your child develop dramatic play means, quite literally, getting down on the floor beside him and really joining in the play – not as an adult instructing the child what to do, but as a participant in the play. For example, instead of saying, 'Look John, this is how we put the doll to bed, the car in the garage, etc.,' it may be more effective if you start by putting yourself in role, saying something like:

'Oh, baby's crying. Oh, poor baby. I think she wants to go to bed. Oh, you don't want mummy to put you to bed, you want John to put you to bed. I think dolly wants you to put her to bed, John. Come on, I'll help you, etc.'

In this way you are establishing that you and your child are both involved in the play sequence.

A similar principle applies in house, shop or car play. Rather than instruct the child from outside the play, it is preferable, and generally more enjoyable, if you feed the child the information he needs in order to develop his play as part of the actual play sequence. For example, as shopkeeper, you can actually assume that the child is participating in the play even when his participation is, in fact, minimal. In this situation you might say:

> 'Hello, John. Would you like to buy some potatoes? No? Carrots? No? Ah, I know what you want. Give me your shopping bag. (take bag from him if he doesn't offer it. Mime putting goods into it.) You want a nice red apple. There you are. I've put it in your bag. That will be ten pence, please. Thank you, John. Goodbye.'

Throughout the entire sequence you may have done all the pretending and John may have contributed virtually nothing. If, however, he has continued to watch you throughout the sequence, and if such sequences are repeated fairly regularly there is a good chance that, at some point, he will begin to contribute to the play. Even if his initial response is merely to nod or to point at something, this is a sign that he is beginning to understand what the play is about. Children who are more advanced, of course, will be able to join in the play. They may not be able to use vocabulary like apples, carrots, etc., but, by hearing these repeated they may become more familiar in the context of play, and, eventually, the child will begin to use them in his own play.

GAMES TO IMPROVE ARTICULATION

Many handicapped children, especially Down's syndrome children, have a dual problem in the development of language. They may have difficulty not only in understanding the spoken word and in expressing themselves in words, but they may also find it difficult physically to use their lips, tongues and other parts of the vocal mechanism in a sufficiently flexible way to give any clarity to their articulation. The games which follow can provide a simple, enjoyable means of giving children practice in using their vocal mechanism, without the complexity of having to use language. They also provide opportunity for practice in early dramatic play.

Blowing

The pursing of the lips involved in blowing can be very difficult for some children. Since this movement is essential in many speech sounds, practice can be helpful.

Bubbles: Start by showing how *you* blow real bubbles with a wand and tin of bubble mixture. At first, simply encourage the child to look at/try to touch/burst/catch the bubbles. Once he has become interested in this he may be willing to try to blow for himself, with you holding the rod and solution. Once he has had practice with real bubbles, blowing imaginary bubbles can be introduced as part of dramatic play. Since you don't have to worry about bursting these bubbles or spilling the liquid, the imaginary bubble-blowing can be a larger, more forceful activity than that involved in the real experience, thus giving more practice in the necessary lip movements. Moreover, the blowing can be combined with movement work involving jumping up to catch the bubbles, running after them, bursting them, etc.

Blow-Football: If no blow-football set is available, two large flexible plastic straws and a ping-pong ball can give the same effect. Again,

> introduce the real activity first and, on
> subsequent occasions, introduce the
> imaginary work based on this.

Other blowing exercises: Blowing a windmill; a dandylion
clock; a feather from the hand;
the candles on a cake; a balloon
and keeping it in the air.

Chewing/Biting/Licking

Again, these are all essential movements in the development of flexible vocal mechanisms. These movements are particularly useful if they are done in an exaggerated and controlled way. Therefore, it is probably better to introduce these movements, from the start, as part of an imaginative activity, rather than to start by using the real objects which the child might chew, lick, bite, etc. For example, suggest to the child that you have an ice-cream and that he has one too. Pretend to lick this in a fairly naturalistic way and encourage the child to copy you. When he can do this, make a game of holding the ice-cream at arm's length and trying to reach it with the tongue; holding it out to the side and trying to reach it with the tongue; getting a spot of ice-cream on the nose, then the cheeks or chin, and trying to lick these off. This is a particularly useful exercise for Down's children who may have problems in achieving mobility of the tongue.

Other licking exercises include: licking cream off a cake; stamps to put on a letter; the flap of an envelope; a cat lapping milk.

Chewing and biting can be introduced in a similarly exaggerated way. For example, suggest that you both have a big red apple (perhaps the one bought on the dramatic play shopping trip?). Polish it up, take a big bite and chew. Go on until the apple is finished and then pretend to find a rubbish bin and drop the core into it with a 'plop'. This could be followed up by hand washing, again introducing the sounds of the tap, etc.

Other chewing and biting exercises include: eating sticky toffee; a dog gnawing a bone; a rabbit munching a carrot; a squirrel cracking and eating a nut.

Speech Games

Having practised the physical movements involved in the chewing, biting, blowing exercises, the natural follow up to this is to provide practice in the articulation of single sounds and onomatopoeic words. Some linguists have suggested that the nonsense babbling which small children engage in before they learn to speak, is actually their attempts to trace and memorise the mechanisms of the vocal tract and the organs of speech. This, combined with the auditory feedback they receive from their own voices, helps them identify and become familiar with making the specific sounds which occur in their native language. Many mentally handicapped children go through this babble stage at a much later age, while others seem to miss it out altogether. This may be why some children fail to master the mechanics of speech, and, since this babble stage is important in the production of speech, it is useful if children can be given the opportunity to practise babbling and to learn to enjoy doing so.

Most sounds can be introduced as a component of dramatic play. For example, a game can be made out of getting up in the morning – the 'brr' of the alarm, the 'sh' of the tap running to wash; the 'zzz' of the toothbrush; the 'glug, glug, glug' of the milk being poured onto the cereal, and of course the 'snap, crackle, pop', of the cereal itself. Similar sequences can be built up using other common household tasks and appliances. Here are just a few examples:

brr – food mixer/car/motor bike/phone;
sh – taps running/squeezy liquid being poured/electric kettle boiling;
bbb – washing machine/dryer/pots or ordinary kettle boiling;

mmm – hoover/car/aeroplane;
wh – wind/hair dryer;
beeb/peep – engaged phone/car horn.

And, of course, the favourite, unmistakeable, and unspellable sound of the police car siren, which I can only write as 'nee naw'.

Moving on

A number of the activities already suggested have had an element of pretence in them. As the child becomes more familiar with working on these, it should be possible to introduce a more sustained imaginative element into the work and to increase the amount of pretence involved, while still retaining the simple sound and movement sequences with which the child has become familiar.

For example, the blowing exercises can provide a lead into the following story, which can be acted out very simply, using only the movements already practised.

STORY

Once there was a boy called John. John blew a bubble – wh, wh, wh. A big, big, bubble – wh, wh, wh. It floated up and up and up and then – it burst. Pop. John blew another bubble – wh, wh, wh. It was a big, big, big BIG bubble. It floated up and up and up and then – pop – it burst, too. John had no bubbles left. But he had a balloon. He began to blow up the balloon – wh, wh, wh, wh, WH. It got bigger and bigger – wh, wh, wh – and bigger and bigger – wh, wh, wh – and bigger and bigger and bigger and BIGGER – wh, wh, wh, and then – BANG. What happened? Yes. The balloon burst. Poor John. Now he had no bubbles, and no balloon. He tried just blowing – wh, wh, wh. But that was no fun. Then he remembered something. He went and looked in his toy-box. And he found this (show a windmill). And he blew – wh, wh, wh. But the windmill didn't float away. He blew again – wh, wh, wh. But the windmill didn't burst. It just went round

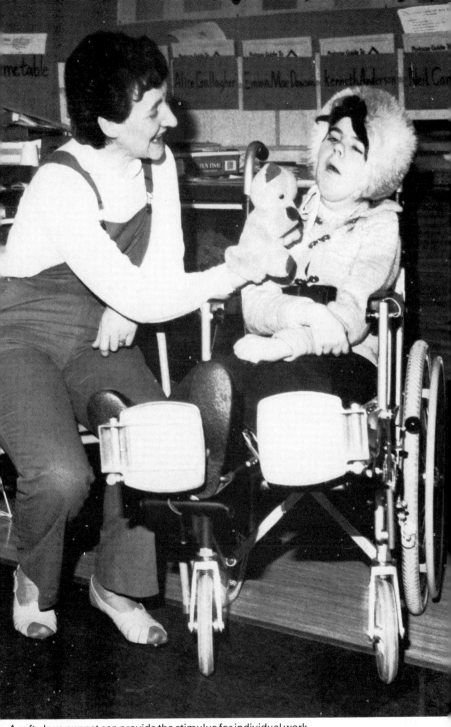

A soft glove puppet can provide the stimulus for individual work.

SPONTANEOUS DRAMATIC PLAY

One of the earliest forms of drama.

he teacher is
the water tray as
ulus for acting
ymes and jingles.

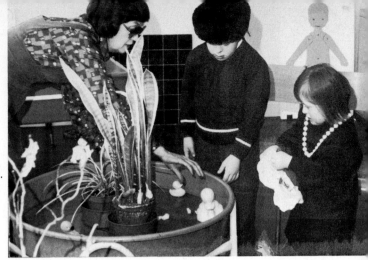

DRAMATISATION

Above: Listening to the story.
Left: Getting ready.

I need a bit
ipstick.
: Acting out the
with the teacher

MUSIC AND MOVEMENT

Exploring the ways in which the body can stretch and push. Chairbound children can join in too.

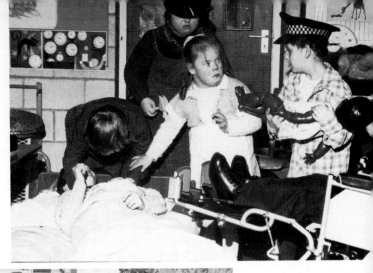

JP
OVISATION

A hospital is a
lace!

Left: Smile please!

: Let's get this
nto jail!

With older children a picture can provide the stimulus for action. Here the children improvise a scene around the theme of the picture.

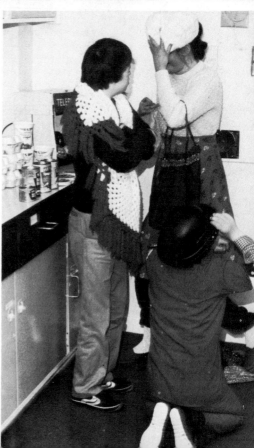

and round and said 'whirr, whirr'. So John was very happy
and he was able to blow his windmill – wh, wh, wh – and
listen to it whirr all day.

Another useful way of consolidating on the sounds and
movements involved in rhymes and jingles is to use these
as a basis for simple acting out. For example, this is a
simple, self-explanatory rhyme which, nevertheless,
allows considerable scope for acting out the making of a
snowman, snowballs, dressing the snowman, etc.

> Come and see. Look at that.
> Our snowman has a scarf and hat. (repeat)

Another rhyme which can provide a great deal of acting
out is the alarm rhyme introduced earlier. Show the child
how to pretend to be asleep and make the sound of the
alarm clock. Show him how to wake up with a start and to
lazily stretch and yawn. When you have established acting
out the waking up part of the rhyme, introduce the part
which signifies bedtime:

> Just before I go to bed (yawn)
> I wind up my alarm (winding clock).
> I pull the covers up to my chin (mime),
> So I'll be nice and warm (yawn).
> Then off to sleep I go (yawn). Like so (fast asleep).

Encourage the child to fit the actions to the words,
exaggerating the yawns (which are another good exercise
for mobility of the speech organs). Eventually the child
should be able to act out the whole rhyme from beginning
to end.

The pussy cat rhyme mentioned earlier also provides a
lead in to such acting out, and, in the bibliography I have
noted a number of books which I have found to be useful
in this context. There are also a number of more advanced
rhymes in the next chapter, and these should provide the
basis for more imaginative dramatic sequences. If your
child has worked through the exercises suggested in this

chapter, he may well be ready to move on to this more advanced work. If he is not, however, he may simply require more practice in the kind of activities suggested here, before moving on.

8 Mime, Movement and Speech

The activities suggested in this chapter are designed to be used with children who have had little previous experience of doing drama, or with those children who already, spontaneously, play at make-believe, but who are just beginning to understand how to act out a role or event in an interactive situation. All of the activities may be carried out either on a one-to-one adult/child basis or within a small group. Much of the material can link fairly directly into the early pre-drama and speech activities suggested in the previous chapter.

Although many of the activities are based on movement, the majority of these may be simply adapted to ensure that wheelchair children are not excluded from the work, and most of the movement work can be done fairly easily by children who only have the use of their upper limbs. Where an activity is really unsuitable for this type of child I have marked it with an asterisk in the text.

Mime and Movement
Mime, as it is practised by celebrated mime artists such as Marcel Marceau, is a highly sophisticated acting technique. For children in the early stages of development, however, mime may be regarded quite simply as acting without words, using gesture and movement, possibly supplemented by sounds, to express the actions or feelings of the characters and the events being portrayed. Mime and movement work is so central to drama with mentally handicapped children (and, of course, with deaf children)

that activities based on these will come into virtually all the practical suggestions given in this book. For example, mime is the central activity in the dramatisation of many of the stories suggested in Chapter Nine, and many of the improvisation ideas given in Chapter Ten will lead on to or develop out of movement. The ideas given here, therefore, are the really simple mime and movement games which help to extend and develop the child's dramatic play.

Speech Games and Rhymes

These are useful in a number of ways. First, they can be used as a means of introducing and reinforcing new vocabulary and encouraging children to make a rhythmic, verbal response. Secondly, they provide practice in the articulation of a whole range of vocal and verbal sounds. Thirdly, and perhaps more importantly, they can link into the work on mime and movement and, by allowing children to combine speech and movement, can provide a simple and effective means of enhancing their enjoyment of the spoken word. Finally, by weaving a simple plot around the repetition of a rhyme, the rhyme may be used as the basis for early dramatisation.

SIMPLE SPEECH AND MOVEMENT GAMES

Game I: Follow my leader

This game gives children practice in giving and responding to instructions. You will need: a number of percussion instruments with different sounds and a tape of lively, rhythmic music.

Stage I Introduce the percussion instruments one at a time. At this stage do not give the children the instruments. Simply demonstrate how to play them, and accompany the sound of each with an appropriate vocal sound, for example 'bang, tap or boom' for a drum, 'ting or ping' for a triangle, 'crash' for cymbals, 'zz' for marakas, etc. Once all the instruments have been introduced and the sounds practised, choose one instrument. As you say the words, play the appropriate instrument and then replace it with the others. The child has then to point to the instrument used. When he gets it right, it becomes his turn to play the instrument and say the words. Once the child can do this easily, ask him to close his eyes. Make the sound of an instrument. The child has to guess which one it is on the basis of sound alone. Speeding up the rate at which you introduce different sounds makes the game fast-moving and fun.

Stage 2   The child should now be familiar with the sounds of the instruments and with the vocal sounds. The child now takes over as leader and the adult has to choose which instrument is being played. An occasional deliberate mistake by the adult can add to the fun of the game for the child.

Stage 3   Dispense with the instruments. Encourage the child to play the game as before, but this time miming the playing of the instrument in time to the appropriate words. The child has guessed correctly if he can either copy the sound heard, or imitate the appropriate movements.

Stage 4   Introduce the taped music. When the music starts both move round the room miming an instrument chosen by the child. When the music stops the adult calls out another instrument. When the music starts again the child moves round miming it. Repeat using a range of different instruments. In a group situation, follow this up by choosing different children to be the leader of the band. When the music stops the leader has to decide what instrument will be played and the other children follow his lead.

Game 2: Mr Men

This is simply an extension of the previous game and is used for the same purpose.

You will need: large pictures of Mr Noisy and Mr Quiet (copied from the Mr Men books by Roger Hargreaves); two cassettes – one with soft gentle music, the other with a loud noisy beat; and additional characters drawn from the Mr Men books, or other men of your own choosing.

Stage 1   Introduce the game by showing the child or children an enlarged picture of Mr Noisy and Mr Quiet. Start the tape. The children have to decide whether the music they hear is that for Mr Noisy or Mr Quiet. When the music is Mr Quiet's they tiptoe around the room saying 'hello' to each other in a whisper. When the music stops they 'freeze' in position. For Mr Noisy's music they stamp around saying 'hello' in the loudest voice possible. Alternate the two at random. Wheelchair children may be able to carry out the exercise by saying the word and clapping hands, tapping their chair or drumming on their knees with their hands, loudly or quietly as appropriate.

Stage 2   ***not suitable for wheelchair children**
Dispense with the music. Put Mr Noisy's picture at one end of the room, Mr Quiet's at the other. The object of the game is to move from one corner to the other, changing from one character to the other as you go. With a group of children, the transition from one character to another may occur as the group from one corner passes the group from the other.

Stage 3   Introduce new Mr Men and encourage the children to mime their actions, for example Mr Bump, Mr Sneezy, Mr Hop, etc. When these have been practised, a child becomes the Mr Man of his own choosing. Other children or the adult say:

How do you do? And who are you?
Mr, Mr, Mr Man show me what you do?

The other children or the adults have to guess which Mr Man the child is miming. With a group, take it in turns to mime and guess.

Game 3: Who am I?

The previous game introduced the idea of miming the actions of a character. This game builds on it by introducing simple occupational mime – the actions appropriate to the occupation of a particular individual.

You will need: pictures of firemen, doctors, milkmen, postmen, policemen, etc.

Stage 1   Introduce the pictures one at a time. Talk about what the people do for us and how they behave. Work at this stage until the child can respond to the request, 'Show me the doctor/show me the milkman/etc.'

Stage 2   Explain that this is a guessing game, and that you are going to be one of the people in the pictures. Say something like:

'Do you know who I am? I come to your house every day and leave a bottle of milk. Who am I?'

If necessary help the child to guess correctly by guiding him to the appropriate picture. When he can guess a number of people correctly, suggest that he could be the character with you, and, demonstrating for him at first, talk him through the actions appropriate to the character.

Stage 3 It is the child's turn to demonstrate the character and your turn to guess who he is. Praise lavishly if you can guess from his actions who he has chosen to be.

Game 4: What Have I Found?

This is simply a variation on the previous game, but instead of 'being' someone carrying out an action, you mime the actions which can be carried out with an object which you have 'found'. Introduce the game in the same way as the previous one using either pictures or real, familiar objects such as a comb, a brush, a lollipop, a lipstick, etc. In this case the child has to guess what it is you have found purely on the basis of your mimed actions, without any additional verbal commentary. When he can do so, take turns at guessing. Obviously, to increase vocabulary, the same game can be played with objects which have been lost, bought, sold, etc.

Speech and Action Rhymes

When a child can carry out the actions and understand the concepts of these games, extend the occupational mime by introducing simple rhymes based on the characters introduced in the games. You will find a number of suitable rhymes in the books mentioned in the bibliography, but I have included some examples here of the kind of rhyme which can be used. Encourage the child to mime the actions as you say the words. Wheelchair children will not be able to join in with all the actions, but they generally enjoy seeing the rhymes acted out by an adult or other children.

1   The milkman drives along the street.
    Then we hear the sound of feet.
    Stamp, stamp, stamp, on the pavements they tramp!
    We hear the bottles clink, clink, clink,
    As he leaves us pints of milk to drink.

Then back to his van –
Goes the milkman.

(Follow this with simple dramatic play in which one child
is the milkman, and another the householder, sleepy,
bringing in the milk for breakfast. With more able children,
follow it with play based on a farm, and the cows who give
us milk.)

2 Early in the morning when the milkman comes to call
   My dog barks – woof, woof.
   When the postman brings the letters and they drop
      into the hall
   My dog barks – woof, woof.
   When my dog hears anyone – ANYONE at all
   My dog barks – woof, woof.
   Woof, woof, woof, woof, woof, woof, WOOF.

(Again, this is a fairly self-explanatory rhyme which can
link in from the previous rhyme and extend into miming the
postman and his occupation. And again it introduces
two characters who have to interact with each other in the
miming.)

3 It was a cold, cold day and the North wind blew.
   Wh, wh, wh, whoooo.
   It blew off my hat, and away it flew.
   Wh, wh, wh, whooo.
   Without my hat what could I do?
   But – atishoo, atishoo,
      atishoo ... A ... A ... A ... Choo.

(With this rhyme you can introduce a more imaginative
element into the work. It can be acted out as it stands, or it
can form part of a larger sequence involving hot drinks to
warm us up after being out in the cold, or a visit to the
doctor or chemist for medicine to cure the cold. This type
of rhyme also provides a basis for introducing simple
dramatisation, the rhyme being repeated several times in
the course of a story about a variety of people who go out,

one by one, to buy some bread. Each one loses his hat and catches cold, and they all end up in the chemist's shop instead of the baker's. A simple repetitive story of this kind can provide a means of repeating the rhyme sufficiently often for children to become familiar with the words and ideas in it without becoming bored.)

DEVELOPING MIME, MOVEMENT AND SPEECH PLAY
Children who have worked through the kind of games suggested above should be ready to go on to more sustained dramatic play based on mime, movement and speech work. The main aims of this form of work are to help the child develop his imagination and to provide him with a topic for conversation – even if, at this stage, he has more gesture than words. The examples given should provide an idea of the kind of work possible at this stage, and of how lessons can be broken down so that they are presented in small, progressive stages similar to those used in the earlier games.

Example 1: Autumn
Remind the children of the sound the wind made in the hat rhyme. Ask them to blow hard like the wind. Then say something like:

'Do you know what happens to the leaves on the trees when the wind blows hard? Yes, they fall slowly down to the ground. Now, I'm going to be the wind and I'm going to blow. And when I blow, you can be the leaves floating gently down to the ground and lying quite still. Try it. I'll blow like the wind and you float slowly, slowly, slowly down to the ground (demonstrate if necessary). And lie quite still. Now, jump up. (Repeat sequence a couple of times.) This time the wind is much stronger. It blows much harder. And the leaves don't fall slowly to the ground, they skip and dance all around as the wind blows them. Could you be the leaves dancing and skipping as the wind blows? Right. The wind is blowing and you are dancing leaves (in a louder voice). The leaves dance all around. And the wind stops (quietly). The leaves stop dancing and float gently, slowly down to the ground. And lie still. The leaves are very stiff. And then they slowly curl up. And lie still.'

With chairbound children it is possible to carry out similar sequences if children use their hands and upper bodies to represent the leaves floating, dancing and lying still, etc.

The following rhyme consolidates the vocabulary introduced in the mime and movement sequence, and allows variation in the work.

> The leaves upon the tree
> Are turning red and brown.
> The wind blows hard – wh–
> And the leaves float down.
> Down, down, down, down, down. (*Getting*
> *quieter on each 'down'.*)

The changing colours of the leaves in the rhyme provide an opportunity to introduce the changes which take place in the texture of the leaves also. Demonstrate, using real leaves, the difference in texture between fresh green leaves and withered brown or red leaves. The rhyme which follows leads into movement work based on this.

> As I walk around
> The leaves on the ground
> Make a crickly, crackly, swishy sound.

Help the children choose different percussion instruments which will illustrate the sound of the leaves being walked on (crickly), jumped on (crackly), and kicked or dragged through (swishy).

The next sequence is unsuitable for wheelchair children. Using the appropriate percussion instruments as background for the movement, the children move through the leaves – walking, jumping or dragging their feet.

Alternate the movements at random. Ask the children to suggest any other ways they might move through the leaves, for example skipping, hopping, running, dancing, etc.

Vary and extend the movement sequences in subsequent lessons to include:

a   Tall trees – stiff and straight; contrast with trees swaying and bending in the wind;

b   Moving gently and slowly, or on tiptoe, to represent a soft gentle breeze; contrast with the forceful rushing movements of a strong wind;

c   Flying kites on a windy day – each struggling to hold the string of his own kite; grouping together to fly a giant kite – all holding same string and moving as a group together;

d   People moving uphill on a windy day, struggling to hold on to hats, skirts, hold up umbrellas or carry heavy shopping bags. Try the sequence in slow motion as an 'action replay', or pretend they are being filmed – every so often the camera breaks down and they have to stand quite still and hold their position until the camera is fixed. Background music helps children in this exercise. (***Less suitable for wheelchair children.**)

e   Stretching up to a high tree to get down conkers; bending low to gather them up; threading them on a string – fine, finger movements; swinging arm movements as they play at conkers. (Examples of real conkers help children understand the ideas presented in the mime sequences.)

f   Shirts being blown on the washing line – floppy arms waving all round; floppy bodies; gradually add trousers, sheets, etc. Encourage the children to move in as relaxed a way as possible as they flop gently in the wind.

g   Introduce the idea that animals go to sleep for the winter, gather food and store it away, etc. Walking through leaves happily then stopping very still to watch a squirrel nibbling a nut and hiding it away; being squirrels gathering, eating and hiding nuts; some children be squirrels, others be humans finding them and standing very still to watch them. Extend to other animals – mice scurrying and eating cheese; hedgehogs extending their spikes – limbs out straight and stiff; hedgehogs curling up into a ball; moving very slowly along the ground, etc.

Example 2: Fireworks

Many of the ideas introduced here can form a direct link with work on autumn. For example, after working on walking, or jumping, through the autumn leaves, you may introduce a lesson based on sweeping up the autumn leaves – large, vigorous arm movements; gathering them up in handfuls – large, enclosing movements of the arms and body; and throwing them in a heap in the middle of the room – expansive, free arm gestures – ready for the bonfire. Follow this up with a mime sequence in which the children collect sticks – stretching up to reach high ones, reaching out to the side, bending low, etc. Tearing up paper and screwing it into a tight ball for the bottom of the fire. Finally *adult* lights fire, children stand well back pretending to keep out of the way of the fire, then dance or skip around the fire.

If this activity is being used to introduce the celebrations for Guy Fawkes night, it presents an opportunity to remind the children, through the play, of the dangers of fire and the fireworks. And these may be incorporated within a mime and movement sequence in which children can practise the safety elements necessary.

Additional movement activities include:

a   Being different kinds of fireworks – round and round for catherine wheels; jumping up in the air for rockets; moving arms to make patterns with small, medium or giant sparklers; jumping as jumping crackers; flames leaping up then dying away and lying still.

b   Encourage the children to make up appropriate verbal or percussion sounds to indicate different kinds of fireworks, or to choose, from a selection of contrasting music, the ones which represent different fireworks (more difficult). Use these to make a tape of background sounds or music. The children should respond in movement to the tape they have helped to make. (This is simpler than it sounds, especially if only one type of firework is introduced at a time and all the aspects of it are discussed and practised separately before introducing another contrasting one.)

c   Follow with an art lesson involving painting the circles, the sweep of the rockets, the wavy patterns of the crackers, etc. Use a very large sheet of paper and either finger paints or very large brushes to encourage free arm movements. Follow the art work with movement work based on painting the fireworks, using the same large, free and expansive movements, and contrast these with flicks of the fingers, arms, wrists, ankles or feet as small sparks fly in all directions.

The fireworks song which follows may help the children remember the words and consolidate the vocabulary introduced in the movement sessions;

> Whoosh go the rockets
> Bang in the sky
> Hear the bonfire crackling
> See the flames leap high
>
> Isn't it fun for us all to remember
> Old Guy Fawkes on the fifth of November
> (repeat first verse)
>
> Fizz go the sparklers
> What a lovely sound
> Catherine wheels keep turning
> Round and round and round
>
> Isn't it fun for us all to remember

Old Guy Fawkes on the fifth of November.
(repeat last verse)

GUY FAWKES SONG

KEY: C MAJOR

It is unlikely that the children at this stage of development will be able to join in the words of this song, but they may very well be able to make the actions to it, and will, almost certainly, enjoy hearing you sing it to them.

Example 3: Hands and Feet (*many of the exercises are not suitable for wheelchair children)

There are a number of rhymes which may be used to introduce finger play or movements such as hopping skipping, jumping, etc. Many of these are to be found in the Clive Sanson books and the other books mentioned in the bibliography. The majority of these, like the action rhymes given in the previous chapter, do not set the movements within an imaginative context. The suggestions given here show how the same range of movements may be extended into more imaginative movement and mime sequences, which involve the child in an element of pretence.

a   Dip hands or feet slowly and tentatively into icy cold water; pulling them back very quickly and sharply as the water touches them.

b   Shake the drops of water off hands and feet – vigorous shaking movements; watch to see where the drops fly – turning heads to look.

c   Walk on soft grass – easy relaxed walking movements; contrast with jerky movements of walking on sharp pebbles.

d   Walk with 'light' feet – skipping movements; contrast with heavy feet – cumbersome, plodding movements, tension in the knees and legs as the feet are moved.

e   Walk on a slippery surface such as ice – using whole body to balance; contrast with walking through deep snow – lifting knees high and replacing feet with sinking movement of the knees.

f   Combine some of the earlier movements in a sequence involving jumping over wet rocks, slipping and sliding on the rocks; finding a rock pool, kneeling to look in it, dipping hands or feet in it – it is very cold – making patterns on the sand with bare feet, walking slowly and carefully, looking for shells, picking them up – fine finger movements for small shells, larger hand movements for big shells or rocks – throwing them into the sea.

g   Walk along happily; you see a large box. It is big and very heavy. Try to lift it, push it, pull it – using hands, knees, elbows, feet, bottoms. It won't move. Kick it. Ouch. That hurt! Hop around nursing your sore toe. Try to open the box. Slowly, slowly. Oh, it opens easily. Look inside. There's a pair of red shoes inside. See if they fit. Try them on. The shoes make you feel funny. They make you want to dance. First your fingers begin to dance very slowly, then your hands, and your arms. Your shoulders begin to dance, slowly, up and down. Your head begins to dance, and your bottom, and your knees. Then your feet begin to dance – very slowly. You dance slowly and quietly – every bit of your body dancing. (Slow sustained music helps here, with the tempo speeding up later. *The Hall of the Mountain King* from the Peer Gynt Suite is very suitable.) Then you begin to dance a little faster, and faster, etc. You are getting very tired. (Reverse the sequence of movement as you slow it down.) You sit down and take off the shoes. Put them back in the box and close the lid. You are so tired you lie down and fall fast asleep.

As many readers will no doubt have observed, a very similar range of sounds and movements comes into most of the exercises introduced in this chapter. And there are a number of reasons for this. First, handicapped children learn slowly. With children who are in the earlier stages of development, it may be necessary to repeat the same range of activities many times before they can fully understand what is being asked of them. By setting the same range of movements and sounds in a variety of different contexts, you can provide children with the amount of practice they need without repeating the same exercises in the same way each time. In this way, lessons can seem fresh and spontaneous and there is less chance of the children (or yourself) becoming bored and losing interest in practising the sounds and movements. Secondly, by introducing the same range of words in different contexts, children can learn to make a wider range of mental associations with these words, and this helps them understand more fully the extent of the meanings of the words involved. Finally, by giving children a chance to repeat the sounds and movements in a variety of imaginative situations, you are helping them to develop a vocabulary of sound and movement with which they may express themselves, both in spontaneous play or in the dramatisation of simple stories such as those which are suggested in the following chapter.

9 Dramatisation

Dramatisation is, as the name implies, the acting out of events and situations which have been presented in the form of a story. Dramatisation of very simple material is quite possible in a one-to-one adult/child situation. In practice, however, dramatisation tends on the whole to be a group activity. It can be a particularly effective method of introducing drama to children who have a reasonably good understanding of language, but who lack the ability to express themselves in words. In both group and individual work, in order to understand and join in dramatisation, the children need to have established some ability to pretend. Children who lack this ability are likely to find it too difficult to make the mental associations needed to link together the characters and events of a story in a meaningful way. For children who can pretend, however, engaging in dramatisation seems to be a useful way of developing the ability to understand cause and effect, and appears to help develop the capacity to order thoughts and actions in a logical sequence.

Dramatisation is a technique which I use a great deal in my own work because I find that many mentally handicapped children react more confidently in a situation which is, to some extent, pre-structured for them by the narrative framework of the story. In dramatising a story the more able children can develop their own ideas of the characters and the way they behave in the situations which have been presented briefly in the story. Less able children can be guided and helped by the prompts provided by the teacher in the narration of the story and by her demonstration of how the characters move, act or speak.

There are no hard and fast rules as to how dramatisation should be presented. Most specialist drama teachers have evolved their own methods of approach. The majority of these, however, are usually personal variations on the four main techniques suggested here. These are:

1   the narrative approach;
2   the 'person-in-role' approach;
3   the open-ended story approach;
4   the guided dramatisation.

Let us look at each of these in turn, and then I will try to show how they differ in practice, using the same story as it might be presented in the different techniques.

THE NARRATIVE APPROACH

This is probably the simplest form of dramatisation and one which I have found particularly useful with the least able children in school. Basically, this approach is simply a re-telling of the story in action. Having told the story once in order to familiarise the children with the characters and events, the adult goes through the story again, expanding and elaborating on the incidents in it and encouraging the children to act these out in unison with her. The children are not given individual parts and do not have to sustain a role in any depth. Rather, they are given practice in trying out a variety of parts in response to the spoken commentary and demonstration of the adult. Like dramatic play, this form of dramatisation is concerned with the events that occur and does not attempt to establish the characters in anything other than a fairly superficial way. Quite literally, the adult talks the children through the various events in the story and encourages them to mime the actions, speak the words, or make appropriate sounds as she does so.

Because there is an emphasis on the events as they occur

in the context of the story, there is less opportunity, in this method, for the children to contribute any of their own ideas as to how the characters might act, move or speak. For able children, this can be a little restrictive, but with less able children, the commentary of the adult, as she demonstrates the actions in the story, can be an invaluable means of encouraging participation and enjoyment – even if the children do not yet fully understand all the niceties of the plot. Because the children are not required to take individual roles, but can act out each role as it occurs in the story, this form of dramatisation lends itself quite well to individual work also.

Moreover, if parts of the story are too complex for the less able children to understand and act out, these can be glossed over or excluded from the dramatisation. Instead, the less complex episodes in the story can be built up into an enjoyable and informative acting-out exercise. For example, in a story a character might go across a road to get to a shop, to post a letter, or to meet a friend, etc. In telling the story such incidents might be presented as a single throwaway line, and the action of the story will not be held up by lengthy explanations of how the character crossed the road, the way he moved while doing so, or what was in his mind as he did so. In dramatisation, however, the simple line 'he crossed the road' could form the basis of a whole sequence of acting out in which the children could practise, in the security of the classroom, all the elements of road safety. Similarly, a phrase like 'he posted the letter' or 'he bought a big bunch of flowers for his mummy' can, in the acting out, be expanded to include many of the elements which might, in reality, be part of such situations. Thus, all the children can act out looking for the hole in the post-box, checking to make sure that their letters have a stamp, making sure the envelope is sealed and addressed, and, finally, dropping it into the post-box with a satisfying 'plop'. All the children can be customers in the flower shop, trying to decide whether to choose roses or daffodils, counting their money to see which they can afford, accepting the flowers, paying for them and carrying them carefully down the busy street. The children can then switch to the role of shop-assistant, selecting the best blooms, perhaps discarding one which is not up to standard, wrapping the flowers carefully, taking the money and opening the till with a 'ping'. Each of these simple, but very enjoyable acting out sequences can be developed and talked through by the teacher as she develops the narrative framework of the story – even if the entire story itself is never acted out within a single lesson. In this form of dramatisation, there is no danger that the 'best' pupils will get the 'best' parts, while others simply have to watch. And this may be a particularly important point in a group where there are a number of very active as well as some rather passive children. I have found that even the most passive children will join in when all the children are working on the same sequence of actions, and, because they can be involved all the time, the more active or distractable children do not become bored.

With less able pupils there is no need to choose a story with enough characters to give everyone a part. Again, this is important because stories for the less able pupils may need to be very simple, with only one or two central characters and only a single incident as the development of the plot. But if only a couple of the children were taking the parts of the central characters in the story, it would be necessary to think up ways of occupying all the others in a group. For example, it might be necessary for most of the children to take the parts of soldiers guarding a palace, trees in a forest, other shoppers in a street, etc. Being one of these extra characters may be fun in its own right, if the teachers ensures that all the children are fully involved in the acting out all of the time and have plenty to do. But if some children are left to stand around 'being trees' while others take the main parts, the 'trees' may get considerably less out of the activity than those with the more active parts.

If, on the other hand, everyone in the group, including

the teacher, is involved in acting out in unison all the main parts, no one is left out and much more detail can be introduced into the sequence of activities.

THE ADULT AS PERSON-IN-ROLE

This is a dramatisation technique which can also be used both in individual and in group work. In this method the adult is not simply the narrator or presenter – demonstrating and guiding the events in unison with the children – but rather adopts a central role in the dramatisation and directs the activity of the children as part of this role. This technique has already been referred to a number of times, and it is certainly a very popular approach with many drama specialists. But it does demand a degree of acting ability on the part of the teacher and, for the inexperienced teacher, may be more demanding than the previous method. On the other hand, there are some children – especially some of the livelier Down's syndrome children – who respond particularly well to this approach.

Again, the story is usually told once in order to set the scene. In the acting out, however, the adult does not retell the story. Rather, she selects from the story one or more central incidents, and uses these to highlight whatever aspect of learning she wishes to establish. For example, in a story involving buying a bunch of flowers the teacher might decide that the learning she wishes to establish is the principle of 'choice' and 'suitability of choice'. Her aim might be to encourage children to make a choice and to think about the appropriateness of that choice in the context of the person who will receive the gift. The teacher might well, therefore, cast herself in the role of the flowerseller, saying something like: 'Ah, now I wonder if some of the people here would like to buy my flowers. I've got red ones and yellow ones. Do you want red ones or yellow ones?' Obviously, this is a very simple choice, and most children will be able to respond to it, even if they can only do so by pointing. However, still in role, the adult may make the choice a more difficult one by suggesting that the red flowers are a very pretty colour, but the yellow ones have a lovely smell. Or she might suggest that for the money the people in the story have available they can buy either a big bunch of yellow, but only a little bunch of red flowers. In this way the children are being forced to make a choice at every stage as part of the dramatic action. The teacher may then introduce the idea of 'appropriateness' – what is the favourite colour of the person who will be the recipient of the flowers in the story? Do the children think she would prefer flowers that have a pretty colour, or ones that have a nice smell? Do they think the character would have a vase big enough to hold the big bunch of flowers, or would she like just a little bunch to set on the little table by her bed? And so on.

The more able children should be able to respond in words to this challenge, especially if the adult feeds them the information in her role. The less able children may have to rely more on the use of gesture to indicate their choice, reaction, etc. With a very able group the teacher might introduce an element of dilemma into the situation. For example, in the scene described above the adult might announce that she only has one bunch of red flowers left and ask the children to decide who should have these on the basis of who (in the story) seems to be the most deserving. With less able children, on the other hand, it may be necessary to provide something concrete which the children can relate to in reality. In the example given above this might mean providing paper flowers, appropriately coloured and scented, as props which will give the children a framework of reality for the imaginative experience of acting out incidents from the story.

As many readers will no doubt have observed by now, this form of dramatisation can be very similar to straightforward role-play or dramatic play. The story merely provides a starting-off point for the development of the dramatic play. But the fact that this play occurs around a story-line makes it easier both for the adult to introduce the activity and for the children to appreciate more easily the context within which the dramatic activity is set.

THE OPEN-ENDED STORY

This is a much more demanding form of dramatisation than either of the others. It is best suited to those children who have had a considerable amount of practice in drama of a simpler kind, and who have well developed imaginative abilities. This is essentially a group activity, and it allows a great deal of scope for children to contribute their own ideas and suggest the direction in which the lesson should go.

As its name implies, this form of dramatisation is introduced in the form of a story which is unfinished. The children themselves are encouraged to decide how the story should develop or end. With this type of work, it may be possible to help the children 'discover' an ending for themselves if the earlier events of the story suggest a fairly obvious way of ending it. With more able children, stories which could have a variety of possible endings provide more of a challenge. In the acting out the children take on different characters, each child deciding for himself who he wishes to be and what his role in the action is. Some of these characters may be ones which have been introduced by the pupils on the basis of their suggestions for developing the activity, rather than simply characters who appear in the original story.

In this form of work the role of the adult is more that of a guide or director than that of the narrator or demonstrator. The adult will feed the children suggestions only when necessary and will accept each suggestion as it is given by pupils and encourage the pupils to act on each suggestion to 'see what happens' in practice. For example, the adult may have told a story about a group of spacemen who have landed on a strange new planet and are exploring it. In the story she may describe something of the landscape, the terrain, the animals, climate, etc., mentioning essential characters like the captain, the cook, the doctor, etc. This feeds in information which the pupils may well use in their later dramatisation. The story itself might stop at the point when the spacemen return to the ship, after a foray on land, only to discover that the ship has disappeared. It is now up to the children to decide who are going to be the various characters needed for the story, and what the next development in the action will be, for example whether they will search for the ship; try to make a home for themselves on the planet; try to radio back to earth for help or rescue; prepare to defend against possible attack, etc. Obviously, if the children cannot provide any suggestions, or cannot agree among themselves on what to try, the adult will feed in extra information and will help the children organise their ideas and action. Whether the adult does this in her role as the teacher, or whether, from time to time, she adopts some kind of role in the drama herself, will be largely a matter of personal preference and the ability of the group concerned. It is perhaps less usual for the adult to take any kind of sustained role in this form of work, but with less able children the teacher may feel that it is necessary to do so in order to help the children work out possible solutions without too much obvious help from her. In general, the more able the group, the less necessary it will be for the teacher to intervene.

Although this is one of the more difficult drama activities for the mentally handicapped child to tackle, and one which calls for a fair degree of self-control, involvement and linguistic ability on the part of the children, it is also one of the most satisfying drama experiences for both pupils and teachers. When it goes well, the children get a real sense of self-satisfaction from having created their own drama out of the story, and the teacher has the pleasure of seeing the children acting creatively or imaginatively without being totally dependent on the ideas she has presented to them.

THE GUIDED DRAMATISATION

In this, as in the previous form of dramatisation, the

teacher's role is that of a guide or leader, helping the children organise and present their own work. In this form of work the adult is unlikely to take any role – other than that of the narrator who links the scenes and provides a continuity in the story-line between the episodes of the drama being enacted.

This is probably the form of dramatisation which teachers are most familiar with. In this form of work the teacher tells the story first. Once the plot and characters of the story have been further established by discussion, the pupils take on the individual parts of the characters in the story and act out in sequence all those episodes of the story which are necessary for the development and resolution of the plot. Generally, the acting out of a story will be accomplished within one lesson, and, having acted it out once, there will be no attempt to polish it or improve upon it. If she wishes to do so, the teacher may provide a few items of clothing or simple props to aid the children in their acting out. These are not necessary in many cases as the children will be quite happy to mime the objects and imagine the clothing. But with less able pupils these simple items of costume or props may help them get the 'feel' of their parts and make it easier for them to become involved in the acting out and play their part with conviction.

This form of sequential dramatisation is, however, fairly demanding on the pupils' imaginative abilities, and their ability to remember and recreate a sequence of actions which are based on cause and effect. Moreover, there is the practical problem referred to earlier of ensuring that the children with less central parts are fully involved and do not stand around for long periods waiting for the time when they will be involved in the central action of the drama.

These, then, are the main forms that dramatisation tends to take. For the children, the simplest is probably the narrative approach or the teacher-in-role situation. The open-ended approach is more demanding on both pupils and teachers. And the guided approach calls for a degree of skill on the part of the teacher in making sure that all the children are fully involved all the time. Incidentally, wheelchair children – providing they can manipulate their upper limbs, and have some independent control of their chairs – ought to be able to join in all these forms of dramatisation without difficulty. Strangely enough, when watching wheelchair children involved in dramatisation, and in many other forms of drama for that matter, it has often struck me that their acting out is so convincing that after a time I do not even notice that they are chairbound.

DRAMATISATION IN ACTION

So far what I have tried to do is to suggest the main ways of tackling dramatisation and the level of difficulty involved in the different methods for both pupils and teachers. I thought it might be useful, however, to give an example of how the same story could be tackled using the four different methods identified, so that readers can judge for themselves which approach seems best suited to their needs. The story I have chosen is one which has been a favourite of mine for a number of years. It has been altered and adapted from time to time to suit different groups. The version given here is the one I use most often, and I have tried to write it more or less as I would tell it to the children. But, as everyone has their own individual storytelling style, the words given here may not suit others. If so, feel free to adapt, change and cut the story as you wish, in order to make it better suited to the abilities, the needs or the environmental situation of your pupils.

The Story: Jim and his Little Red Car

Once there was a man called Jim. Jim lived in a town. Every day when he got up in the morning, Jim would open the window and just stand there listening to the lovely town sounds all around him. Peep! peep! That was the sound of a car horn. Brrr. Brrrrr. A big red bus rumbled by.

Neenaw, neenaw, neenaw, neenaw! Jim knew what that noise was! It was a police car racing down the street.

Jim liked living in the town and listening to the noises of the town. He liked driving his little red car through the busy streets when he went to work in the morning. And he liked driving it home again at night after his work was done. But Jim liked it best of all on Saturday, when he didn't need to go to work and when he could drive his little red car up and down the streets all day if he wanted to.

One Saturday Jim got into his little red car and drove off. He drove up the road, round the corner, down the hill and all over town. He was so happy he sang to himself as he went. (Any appropriate song here. I generally use 'the wheels on the car go round and round', or one of the motor rhymes from the Clive Sansom books mentioned in the bibliography.) Jim was so busy singing and driving, and driving and singing, that before he knew what he was doing he drove the little red car right out of the town and down a little windy road. And in the middle of that little windy road there was some thick, brown sticky mud. The little red car drove right into the mud and stuck there. Jim tried to get the little red car to move, but it was no use. The engine went brrr, brrrr and the wheels went round and round, but the little red car wouldn't move.

Along came a black car. Peep, peep, peep, peep.

'Stop,' said Jim, and he held up his hand like a policeman. 'Stop.' The black car stopped.

'What's wrong?' asked the driver of the black car.

'It's my little red car. It's stuck in the mud and it won't move.'

'I'll help you push,' said the driver of the black car. And so they pushed. They pushed and they pushed. But the little red car didn't move.

Along came a bus – brrr, brrrr, peep, peep, peep.

'Stop,' said Jim. The bus stopped and the driver got out.

'What's wrong?' asked the driver of the bus.

'It's my little red car. It's stuck in the mud and it won't move.'

'We'll help you push,' said the bus driver. All the people in the bus got out to help to push, too. They pushed. And they pushed. And they pushed. But the little red car didn't move. Then everyone heard a noise. Neenaw, neenaw, neenaw. Yes! It was the police car. The police car stopped.

'What's wrong here?' asked the policeman.

'It's my little red car. It's stuck in the mud and it won't move.'

'Hmmm,' said the policeman. 'I think we can help you.'

The policeman tied a rope to the front of the little red car. Then he tied the other end of the rope to the back of the police car.

The policeman started the engine of the police car – brrr, brrrr. And the police car started to pull. It pulled and it pulled. And all the people pushed and they pushed. And the wheels of the little red car went round and round. And the little red car moved right out of the mud.

'Hurray,' cheered all the people.

'Oh, thank you,' said Jim.

'That's all right,' said the policeman. 'Come on, we'll lead you back into town.'

So Jim got into his little red car. The driver of the black car got into his car. The policemen got into their car. And the bus driver, and all the people, got back into the bus.

'Goodbye,' said Jim, 'and thank you.'

'Goodbye,' said all the people, and they waved.

Then Jim drove very carefully all the way back into town behind the police car which said neenaw, neenaw, neenaw, all the way.

The Story Dramatised in the Narrative Form

Since the narrative form is likely to be used with younger or less able children, or in individual work with a single child, it is a good idea to prepare the children for the story before telling it. I usually do this by encouraging the children to sing the song and mime the actions of it before telling the story. This helps familiarise children with the sounds and words they are going to hear in the story itself.

This preparatory work might take one or two lessons. The telling of the story would take up another lesson, but in telling the story I pause from time to time and invite children to join in some of the words and actions as they occur, for example the car noises; the word 'stop'; the pushing and pulling. I would not, at this stage, ask the children to move out of their seats, but would simply expect them to join in the story from where they are sitting listening to it.

In the next lesson the children are reminded of the story. All of them then become Jim and act out, in some detail, the events of the morning: being asleep, waking up, teeth cleaning, breakfasting, and, finally, listening to the town noises and making these. This forms an entire lesson, and, at the end of the lesson I ask the children to suggest other noises they might hear in the town, and to try making these. A further lesson can involve the sequence where Jim drives his car, sings the song, gets stuck in the mud, and tries to push. The next lesson might then be a sequence in which the children button up coats, put on shoes, prepare to catch the bus, etc. As they wait at the bus stop they may find it cold, or wet and have to turn up their collars, pull scarves tighter, put up umbrellas, etc. In another lesson the children can act out, in unison, a number of the policeman roles: directing the traffic, helping people across the road, driving the panda car, and coming to Jim's rescue with their rope. At this point the children may divide into two groups – one to push and one to pull – in order to move the car.

If the children have worked through these sequences in some detail over a number of lessons, they should be pretty familiar with the characters and actions involved in the story. It is perfectly possible to go on to new work without ever acting through the entire story sequence. With a fairly able group of pupils, however, I tend to move on to the 'guided' approach at this stage and allow them to act out the story, taking individual parts and working on the appropriate actions.

The Teacher-in-role Version

This story is not particularly well suited to this approach. When using the teacher-in-role method it is best to choose a story in which there is a central character who is in a position of some authority or importance and whose words and actions act as a directive or guide to the children. Jim is the central character in this story, but there are few occasions in the story where he is in an authoritative or directing role. If, therefore, the teacher were to choose to be Jim, while the other children took the other parts, the teacher would have to rely on the children carrying out their parts without prompting from her and this negates much of the interactive value of this method of work.

On the very few occasions when I have taken a role in this story, I have generally cast myself in the role of a traffic policeman. In this role I was free to move around to some extent, and was able to direct the activity of the children's 'cars' and 'buses'. I could quickly follow up their actions by arriving at the scene of the problem and could then show them how to help me by pushing the car, tying the rope, standing well back, etc. This worked reasonably well but it is much simpler to adopt the teacher-in-role approach when all the action of a story takes place in the one setting, and there are other stories which lend themselves much better to this approach than the story we have been considering here.

The Open-ended Form of the Story

When using this approach I end the story at the point where the car is stuck in the mud and the children are asked to suggest and try out different ways of getting it out. It is impossible to predict in advance how the story and the acting out will develop at this point since each group of children will have their own ideas as to what might be tried, and the range and quality of these suggestions will depend to a large extent on the imaginative and linguistic ability of the group in question.

Some of the suggestions which children have given me
include: getting the farmer's horse to pull the car out (the
children had been working on the theme of the farm and
particularly liked making animal and clip-clop noises);
getting a crane and bulldozer and, amid much buzzing and
creaking noise, lifting the car out of the mud (this
suggestion came from a group of boys, naturally); digging
the car out with spades; leaving the car and going home to
phone the AA (from an intelligent, but very disturbed
child); everybody getting stuck in the mud one by one till
nobody could move at all. This last sequence was
suggested and carried out by a group of mildly
handicapped pupils. It was hilarious and completely
chaotic, and the only thing that finally persuaded them to
abandon their imaginary mud bath was the ringing of the
interval bell. If the children are lacking in ideas and you
wish to introduce some, I suggest that this last idea be used
with caution – unless, that it, you think you can cope with
the chaos it will almost certainly bring.

The Guided Dramatisation
First, either work through the kind of sequences suggested
above, or, tell the story and allow plenty of time for
discussing the sequence of events, the characters and the
sounds in the story. In the next lesson remind the children
of these, discuss with them (or suggest) where the various
locations in the story are going to be placed in the
classroom. Set out chairs, etc., in position for the various
vehicles. The children can then decide which parts they
are going to play. They take their places in the various cars.
I find it tends to work best when the acting out starts at the
point where Jim is stuck and is trying to get out of the mud.
This prevents children having to wait around until it is
their turn for the action as, from this point in the story, the
action moves quickly and all the children can be involved
more or less all the time. I generally finish it off by having
all the children get back into their cars and sing the song as
they wave goodbye to each other.

CHOOSING A STORY TO DRAMATISE

Which method you choose for dramatisation will obviously depend to some extent on your own personal teaching style, and on the level of ability of the children in your charge. No one method is intrinsically better than any of the others. and you might well find yourself adopting more than one approach at different times in dramatising the various episodes in a single story. But the story itself may also suggest which method of dramatisation is likely to be most appropriate. As one might expect, the least able children often respond best to very simple stories in which there are only a few characters, a simple familiar setting, only one episode in the plot, an emphasis on sound and movement, and, possibly, repetition of a line of dialogue or a rhyme within the story. The narrative and guided approaches are often best for this type of story. With more able pupils the story chosen might well have an emphasis on sound and movement, but the plot itself can be more complex and less tied to reality. If, in addition, the story has a strong central character and a reasonably simple setting, the teacher-in-role approach may well be appropriate. With the most advanced pupils, stories may have a strong humorous or fantasy element and the setting may be one which is considerably removed from that of the children's everyday lives. Any of the above methods may be suitable, but if the development of the plot has an obvious break-point in it, it may be possible to use the open-ended approach by stopping the story at that point. Incidentally, I often find that, after their own dramatisation, children enjoy hearing how the story 'really' ends and comparing their own ideas with the author's.

All teachers have their own favourite stories, many of which will probably lend themselves quite well to dramatisation. However, just to give an idea of the type of story which I have found useful for dramatising with different groups of mentally handicapped children, I have included a few examples, together with an idea of their level of difficulty, and a possible method of dramatisation. Additional stories are suggested in the bibliography.

Stories

The Birthday Present

Margaret was very happy. It was her birthday. She had a big box of chocolates from her Aunt Jean. Her mum and dad gave her a red tricycle with a bell, and from her friends she got lots of books and toys and crayons. But Margaret was puzzled. She always got a lovely birthday present from Grandpa. But today she hadn't got anything from Grandpa. It was very strange.

Margaret had a lovely birthday. She had a birthday tea with her friends. They played games, and they blew up balloons, and they had lots of sweets, and crisps, and sandwiches and cakes and sausage rolls to eat. When all her friends went home, Margaret helped her mummy to wash up the dishes. Just then the front door bell rang. When mummy came back from answering the door she was carrying a parcel.

'That was the postman,' mummy said, 'I think this must be your present from Grandpa.'

Margaret was pleased. Grandpa hadn't forgotten her birthday after all. She tore off the brown paper, and inside there was a box – a cardboard box. Inside the cardboard box there was another box – a wooden one this time, with pictures all round the side and a little handle sticking out in front.

'Oh,' cried Margaret, 'it's a musical box. Do you think Grandpa made it himself?'

'Yes, I'm sure he did,' said her mummy. 'Turn the handle and we'll hear the music.'

Margaret turned the handle and the box began to play:
'Half a pound of tuppenny rice, half a pound of treacle,
That's the way the money goes, pop goes the weasel.'

But when the music got to the words '*pop goes the weasel*', the top of the box flew open and a funny little man with a big red nose and wobbly eyes popped right up out of the box.

'Take it away. Take it away. What is it?' shouted Margaret, because she felt very frightened.

Margaret's mummy laughed. 'There's nothing to be frightened of,' she said. 'Look! it's a jack-in-the-box.' And Margaret's mummy showed her how to turn the handle and make the little man come out every time the music went '*pop goes the weasel*'. Soon Margaret wasn't at all afraid and she began to laugh every time the little man popped out. In fact she liked her jack-in-the-box so much that she played with it all evening until it was time for bed.

'I think Grandpa is very clever to make such a good present, 'said Margaret.

I think so too, don't you?

It is useful to have a real jack-in-the-box as a visual aid for this story. Dramatisation is likely to be of the narrative type, with no attempt to recreate the entire sequence of the story. The party sequence and the opening of the parcel are generally much enjoyed. I generally follow or precede this story with movement work in which the children become a jack-in-the-box and other, contrasting toys.

Sports Day

Mr and Mrs Brown were getting ready to go out. They were going to the park. It was a nice day so Mr Brown put on his brown jacket. Mrs Brown put on her new red coat. And off they went round the corner and up the hill to the park.

Mr and Mrs Brown passed the duck pond where the ducks were swimming around. They passed the red bench where they liked to sit down. And they walked on through the park.

Suddenly, Mr and Mrs Brown heard voices. They were

children's voices and they were shouting, 'Hurray, hurray. Come on John. It's a goal. Hurray.' Mr and Mrs Brown hurried on. What could be happening in the park today?

The children from Hightown School were in the park. It was the school's sports day. Some of the children were standing watching the others and cheering. Some were running races. Different kinds of races. The sack race. The potato and spoon race. The three-legged race and the wheelbarrow race. Some of the children were jumping. And two teams of boys were playing football.

Mr Brown liked football. He liked to watch it on television. But he liked it even better when he could be at the game. Mr and Mrs Brown stopped, and they stood beside a big tree to watch the children playing football. It was a good game. First, the blue team scored a goal. 'Hurray,' shouted the children who were watching. Then one of the red team tried to score. But the goalkeeper was too good for him. He caught the ball and threw it back onto the pitch. 'Ah,' said the children who were watching. The red team was coming forward again, and one boy was running with the ball at his feet. He kicked, and he scored! The red team had scored a goal too. The referee blew his whistle. Wheee. The game was over. It was a draw – two all.

The football match was finished. The races were finished. And so was the jumping. The school's sports day was over, and all the children packed up and went back to school.

Mr and Mrs Brown decided to go home too.

'I enjoyed that football match,' said Mr Brown. 'Did you?' Mrs Brown didn't say anything. She just smiled. I wonder if she did enjoy it? What do you think?

The incidents in this story need space for the acting out, so it is probably better to dramatise a story like this in the hall rather than in the classroom. There may be rather a lot of unfamiliar vocabulary in it too, so the children may need some of the terms explaining and demonstrated to them, for example the wheelbarrow race; the referee; the pitch, etc. Encourage the children to talk about the sporting events they have taken part in or seen on TV, invite discussion on whether they think Mrs Brown had enjoyed the game, and why. This story is definitely not suited to dramatisation by the person-in-role and open-ended approach. Either of the other two methods could be used. I find a story like this is much more effective when taken as part of a larger theme – for example, the ball theme given on pp. 91–104. Often I simply use the story as a lead in to the acting out of a series of movement based work, and it can be followed by art-work in which the children choose their own team colours and create a collage of footballers dressed in the colours they have chosen.

Peter the Postman

Peter the postman liked his work. He liked delivering letters and parcels and postcards to all the houses in the village. At least he liked it in the summertime when the sun shone and the weather was warm and sunny. He even liked it on a cold, dark winter's morning. But he definitely did not like it on the days when the rain came down and he could feel his feet and his jacket getting wetter and wetter and colder and colder as he walked all over the village delivering his letters.

One day, it was so wet that Peter the postman did something he had never done before. He just didn't go to work at all! He lay in his warm bed and listened to the noise of the rain outside. But he didn't go to work. And that morning nobody in the village got any letters.

The next day it was raining again. And again Peter the postman stayed in bed. He wasn't ill. He just didn't go to work. And nobody in the village got any letters that day either.

Mrs Smith at the Post Office phoned Peter the postman.

'You must come to work,' she said, 'I've got a pile of letters and parcels and postcards for you to deliver.'

'It's raining,' said Peter the postman. 'I don't like the rain. It makes me all wet. So I'm not coming back to work till the rain stops.'

Now Peter the postman had never done anything like this before. And Mrs Smith didn't know what to do. 'You must come to work,' she said again.

But Peter the postman didn't answer. He just put down the telephone and went back to sleep.

All that week the rain came down. And all that week nobody in the village got any letters or parcels or postcards. Then Mrs Smith called a meeting in the village hall. Everybody in the village came to the meeting. They all tried to decide what to do to get Peter the postman to come back to work in the rain. At last they had an idea.

Early the next morning Peter the postman heard a knock on his door. When he opened the door it seemed as though everyone in the whole village was standing outside in the rain. Then Mrs Smith stepped forward.

'We've brought you a present, Peter,' she said. 'Please open it and then come back to work. We need you to deliver all our letters.'

She held out the parcel. Peter looked at it for a moment. And then he opened it. Inside the parcel was a big pair of black wellington boots, and a big black waterproof cape with a hood. Peter didn't say a word. He pulled on the big black wellington boots. Then he put on the big black waterproof cape and pulled up the hood. He stepped outside into the rain and he stood there, still saying nothing. Then he smiled.

'Thank you for the present,' he said. 'Now I won't get wet any more. I think I'll come to work today after all.'

He closed the door and walked, in the rain, all the way down to the Post Office. Everyone in the village gave a great cheer, and then went back home.

Now Peter the postman goes to work every day, and he doesn't mind the rain. And the people in the village get their letters every day, too, no matter what the weather is like.

As it stands this story is particularly suitable for dramatisation by either the guided or person-in-role approach. If choosing to use the role approach, it is probably better if the adult takes the role of Mrs Smith, rather than Peter. Although Peter is the central character in the story, it is Mrs Smith who is the pivotal point on whom the action hinges, and she is in a much better position than any of the other characters in the story to direct and control the action. If using the guided approach, there are plenty of parts for all the children as villagers, and the teacher can build these parts up by suggesting what the villagers are doing when their letters come – and then don't come. The meeting in the village hall, and the subsequent walk to Peter's house, or the purchase of the present, all give plenty of scope for the whole group to be involved in a sequential acting out of this story.

With more able pupils this story is an ideal one for the open-ended approach also. The story can be stopped at the point where the decision has to be taken about what to do to get Peter back to work. And the suggestions given by the children can be tried out in turn. If, using this approach, an additional adult is available to act as Peter, this will provide the children with a real dilemma as they will be unable to know in advance how Peter is going to react to the actions they try. Alternatively, the teacher herself may take the role of Peter, but this is more difficult to manage in that the children then have to take the responsibility for their own action in relation to Peter and this calls for a fairly high level of ability on the part of at least some of the children in the group.

The Stray Kitten

Mrs Jones was an old lady. She lived by herself in a tiny flat at the bottom of a big block of flats in a busy town. Mrs Jones liked her little flat because she had lots of friendly neighbours who often came in to visit her and to have a cup of tea and a chat. But there were some days when no one came to visit her. On these days Mrs Jones felt very lonely and she wished she had a friend to keep her company.

One lonely day Mrs Jones was washing the dishes at the sink by her kitchen window, when she heard a noise. Miaow. Miaow. It sounded like a cat. Miaow. Miaow. Mrs Jones was sure it was a cat. She pulled back the curtain from the window and looked out. Miaow, Miaow. It was a cat! A furry little black cat with one white paw and one white ear. It was looking at her through the kitchen window and miaowing as if to say, 'please take me in. It's very cold out here. And I'm hungry. Please take me in and give me some milk.'

Mrs Jones opened the window. In one minute the little black cat was inside the kitchen and standing by the fridge. In two minutes Mrs Jones had taken a bottle of milk from the fridge and put some of the milk into a saucer. In three minutes the little cat had lapped up a whole saucer of milk and was miaowing for more. Five minutes later Mrs Jones was sitting in her favourite chair with a little black stray cat on her knee. The cat was purring – prrrr, prrr. And Mrs Jones was smiling.

That was a long time ago. But if you were to go and visit Mrs Jones today, do you know what you'd see? Yes! Mrs Jones would be sitting in her favourite armchair with a little black cat on her knee. The cat would be purring – prrr, prrr – because he was happy to have found a good home. And Mrs Jones would be smiling, because even on the days when no one comes to visit her, Mrs Jones is never lonely now. She has her little black cat as a friend to keep her company.

This is the simplest of all the stories given so far. As there are only two characters in the story, it is particularly well suited to individual work with a single child. I find that the cat rhyme and cat movement suggested on pp. 119 and 129 make a useful link between this story and the movement and sounds involved in the dramatisation of it. The dramatisation itself is likely to be the narrative type which allows all the sequences and actions in the story to be expanded and elaborated on, while the actual dialogue necessary is minimal.

More Advanced Stories

The story which follows is not particularly difficult to dramatise using either the narrative or open-ended method. In the case of the latter, the story would stop at the point where Allan is feeling unhappy and doesn't know what to do. Some of the words in the story are, however, fairly difficult, and the concept of the plot may be a difficult one for the less able children to grasp. It is for this reason that it has been suggested as a more advanced activity than those presented so far.

The Dragon that Nobody Liked

One Saturday morning Allan was looking at a book. The book was called *The Dragon that Nobody Liked*. There was a picture of a dragon on the front of the book. The dragon had a big red tongue and smoke was coming out of its nose. The picture of the dragon gave Allan an idea. He went into the kitchen.

'Look at me, look at me,' he called to his Mummy and Daddy.

'I'm a dragon. Grrrrrrrrrr.' And he ran around the kitchen and made what he thought was a loud dragon noise. But Mummy and Daddy didn't seem to like it much.

'Don't be silly, Allan,' said Mummy. 'Go and play. Daddy and I are busy.'

Allan went upstairs. His sister Susan was in her bedroom writing.

'Look at me, look at me, Susan. I'm a dragon,' cried Allan, and he made his dragon noise again. 'Grrrrr.'

'Oh, don't be silly, Allan,' said Susan. 'Go away. Can't you see I'm busy?'

Allan went out into the garden. His brother Mark was fixing his motor bike.

'Grrrrr. Grrrrrr. Look at me. I'm a dragon.'

'Oh go away, Allan,' said Mark. 'I'm busy.'

Poor Allan. He went back into the house. He looked at his book again. *The Dragon that Nobody Liked*. That's just like me, thought Allan, no one likes me either. Everyone's too busy to play with me. Allan sat and felt sorry for himself for a little while. He was unhappy and he didn't know what to do. And then he had an idea. He took a sheet of paper out of his drawing book. Then he took his new felt-tip pens. And he began to draw. His Mummy came in.

'What's that you're drawing, Allan?' asked Mummy.

'A dragon,' said Allan.

'It's a very good dragon,' said Mummy. 'I like it.' His Daddy came in.

'What's that you're drawing, Allan?' asked Daddy.

'A dragon,' said Allan.

'It's a very good dragon,' said Daddy. 'I like it.' Susan and Mark came in together.

'What's that you're drawing, Allan?' asked Susan.

'A dragon,' said Allan.

'It's a very good dragon,' said Susan.

'Yes, I like it,' said Mark.

Allan finished his drawing. Then he looked at his family. After a while he smiled.

'Yes,' he said,' I think it is a very good dragon. It's the dragon that everyone likes!'

With children who are at this slightly more advanced level it is possible to use many of the traditional tales. Stories such as *The Three Little Pigs*, *The Tale of a Turnip*, *The Princess and the Pea*, and many of the *Naughty Little Sister* stories by Dorothy Edwards can be used with very little adaptation to suit the mentally handicapped child. And all of these stories provide a very good basis for dramatisation.

Some of the traditional fairy tales, such as *Snow White*, *Hansel and Gretel*, *Cinderella* or *The Sleeping Beauty*, can also be used with children who are well enough advanced imaginatively to be able to understand the fantasy element in these. Since most of the published versions of these stories tend to be rather long, and to contain many words which are likely to be unfamiliar to handicapped children, I find it better to tell, rather than read, these. In this way, it is possible to modify and adapt both the plot and the language to make them more simple, and more suitable for the children's enjoyment. In dramatising these stories, I find that it is generally better to select episodes from the stories for dramatisation rather than to attempt to dramatise the whole story, as the stories themselves are complex to act out, both in the language used and in the variety of settings introduced. In the bibliography I have suggested a number of other stories and story books which contain ideas that are particularly useful for developing through dramatisation.

Finally, with the most able children there may come a time when you would like to take the dramatisation a step further than classroom drama and turn it into a more polished dramatisation which could be presented to others. If you are working with a group of children who appear to be ready and able to engage in a performance of this kind, the last chapter shows how a simple classroom dramatisation may be extended to provide the basis for play-making and performance.

PART THREE

More advanced activities for use in
developing regular drama
programmes

10   Role-Play and Improvisation

Earlier, when we were looking at the kinds of drama work suitable for different groups of children, it was suggested that dramatic play could be regarded as the acting out of events and situations, role-play the acting out of the feelings and personalities of characters, and improvisation as an amalgam of the two with, perhaps, more emphasis on dialogue. In Chapters Seven and Eight I suggested the kind of early dramatic play, mime, movement and speech activities which might be suitable for the developmentally younger child. In this chapter I should like to concentrate on some of the role-play and improvisation exercises that are more suitable for children who are developmentally more mature, and who have already established the ability to pretend.

SIMPLE ROLE-PLAY

Up to about the age of seven or eight non-handicapped children tend to see characters as stereotypes: the policeman is the man who catches thieves, or the man who waves his arms to control the traffic; the doctor is the man who gives us medicine and makes us better, and so on. These characters are not seen as real people but as a symbol of what they do. In the early stages of developing role-play, this view of people as stereotypes will be reflected in the children's play. They will not tend to differentiate between the characters they are acting except in very crude terms. The 'angry' person will be characterised only by anger and by no other dimension of the personality. Similarly, the personalities of doctors, policemen, dentists, etc., will be ignored and the characters will be represented simply by the actions seen as appropriate to their occupational roles. And the roles which the children adopt in their spontaneous play are likely to be those, either of people with whom they are familiar, or whose behaviour has recently attracted their attention and interest.

Similarly, in early role-play situations within the drama lesson, it is sufficient for the children to act out these rather superficial and stereotyped characters, and to grasp the concept that society is made up of different occupational groups, each performing a different function within their occupational roles. The simplest form of role-play is, therefore, occupational mime, often with an adult demonstrating the various occupational tasks which different people might perform.

As mentally handicapped children mature more slowly than non-handicapped children, it would be perfectly acceptable for children of ten, twelve, or even older, to portray characters in the stereotyped form of occupational mime, and to portray, in the drama lesson, the occupational groups with whom they are most likely to come in contact in their daily lives. Once children have gained some practice in acting out these familiar roles, however, they may be ready to move on to more complex role-play situations in which they are encouraged to extend their acting out to characters which are less familiar, or to characters in rather more unusual settings. Initially, these less familiar characters and settings may still be portrayed in occupational mime, and it is only the developmentally mature children who will be able to think of people in terms of their problems, conflicts and personalities.

Some Examples of Simple Role-Play

1   Each child is one of a team of workmen. They are
    clearing up the dead leaves, mowing the grass, re-

planting the flowerbeds, etc. in the park after the winter is over. If necessary, the adult can help organise the children's activity by taking the role of park-keeper, and instructing the workmen on the tasks which have to be done.

2   Each child is a hairdresser in a busy salon. Each child has his own customer and shampoos, sets and cuts hair, etc. If necessary, talk the children through the various tasks in unison, before asking them to take individual roles. Again, the adult may adopt a supervisory role, encouraging children to explain, in role, what they are doing to their customers.

3   When the children have practised being hairdressers with an imaginary customer, they may, with adult help, be able to work in pairs, each sustaining a role as either customer or hairdresser. This work may be developed into a simple play in which something 'happens': for example the perm goes wrong; the customer does not like the style; a very 'special' customer comes in, etc.

4   Working in pairs, one child is a television camera man making a film for a television series, while the other child is being filmed carrying out some task. For example, he could be trying on different hats; modelling clothes; baking a cake; showing how to paint a picture or paper a room, etc. The camera man tries to film from as many different angles as possible. (As this is a fairly complex activity, it may be necessary for the children to work in unison at first – all being camera men, then all being the model. If they have practised the individual roles in this way they ought, eventually, to be able to combine them when working as pairs.)

5   An angling competition. Each child is an angler, trying to catch a large fish with a rod and line. Some fish may be too small and have to be thrown back. Some fishermen may have to wade into the river. Others may

cast their lines from the bank, but may not have much success, etc. It is helpful if the adult talks the children through this activity, making suggestions which will extend the children's ideas of how the characters act.

6   As a follow on from the previous activity, the children could be different kinds of fishermen – deep sea fishermen in a boat, fishing with nets instead of rods and working as a team to cast the nets and haul them in. This may lead to pairs work in which one child is a customer, the other a shopkeeper in a fishmonger's, or perhaps a fish and chip shop.

More Imaginative Role-Play

Once children have grasped the concept of sustaining an individual role, and have practised acting out a role in fairly familiar settings, they may be able to move on to situations in which the settings for the characters are more imaginative. For example:

1   It is Hallowe'en. Each child is a witch, baking a 'nasty' cake to take to the witch's ball. Encourage the children to decide for themselves what kind of 'nasties' they are going to put in their cakes, the words they are going to use in the spells they cast over them, and the effect which the cakes will have on anyone who eats them. With some children it may be necessary to precede this activity with occupational mime based on the baking of a real cake, in order to give them a vocabulary of words and actions on which to base the more imaginative work. With an able group the actual witch's ball, or the effects of the cakes being eaten, could form subsequent role-play sessions, and the whole sequence could be developed into a more structured classroom drama play.

2   Villagers have been told that a Prince is coming to visit their village. All the different people in the village are going to prepare a special welcome for him. Each child

decides on his role, for example, the mayor, the
schoolmaster, the baker, the painter, the roadworkers,
etc. The children may need considerable help in
discussng who the various people in the village are,
and what each could do to contribute to the Prince's
special welcome. Having discussed this, each child
then acts out his own part in the preparations. Or the
children might decide to work together – decorating
the street with flags and flowers, etc. The adult may
either help the children organise their own activity, or
may take the role of the Prince and engage the children
in conversation about, for example, who made the
beautiful cake/gathered the flowers/made the roads so
clean/painted the houses, etc. By encouraging the
children to talk about their part in the activity in this
way, the adult is helping them to sustain and develop
their roles further.

3   Working in pairs, one child is Doctor Who, and the
other a robot he is making. The children build up their
robots and when they are ready, stand back to look at
them. Then something goes wrong – for example, the
robot goes slower and slower and finally breaks down;
it will not respond to instructions; it starts to perform
the same task over and over, regardless of instructions;
it goes in the wrong direction or moves too quickly, etc.
This is a fairly sophisticated role-play scene and there
may be some children who find it difficult to know how
to develop their role. If this proves to be the case, or if
you suspect that the children would experience such
difficulty, a simpler version of this play is to have the
children working on imaginary robots, or, better still,
for all the children to be building one robot. In this case
the adult may take the role of the robot and help the
children to respond both by asking them for
instructions, and by the way in which she carries these
out. Appropriate background music also helps create a
suitable mood for this type of activity, and natural

breaks in the music can signify a change of activity or tempo in the work.

More Advanced Role-Play

As children mature they begin to get less satisfaction out of acting stereotyped occupational situations or purely imaginary settings, and begin to take an interest in the real feelings and personalities of different people. Generally, I would expect to find mentally handicapped children developing this degree of maturity around the middle to late teens. And there are likely to be relatively few children in the age-group at which this book is aimed who are ready for the more advanced forms of role-play. Nevertheless, a few of the more able children may be able to tackle these, if they have had plenty of previous practice in the simpler forms of play.

Unlike the simpler forms of role-play, which may be acted out with very little dialogue, the more advanced forms of role-play do require a reasonable linguistic ability and rely less heavily on mime. In the early stages of this work, it may be helpful if the adult initially takes one of the roles in order to interact with the children and give them practice in the kinds of responses that are possible.

1　In pairs, one is a newsagent and the other a child who has been sent to do some shopping. By the time the child reaches the shop he has

either　forgotten the name of the item he had to buy, and the shopkeeper tries to jog his memory;

or　cannot remember where he put the money and the shopkeeper is suspicious as to whether he ever had any money;

or　the items he had to buy are sold out. The shopkeeper suggests alternatives and he has to decide whether or not these might be suitable.

Act out what happens in each case.

2　In pairs, as a follow up to the previous example, one

child is a parent, the other a child. The child tries to explain to the parent what took place in the shop. Act out the scene and show how the parent reacted.

3 In groups of three, three children are playing with toy cars. One steps back and stands on another child's toy, destroying it. How do the children react? If the children act the scene out with anger, etc., suggest that they try it again in another way and find a different solution, for example the child may offer to replace the toy and his offer is accepted; the child whose toy is destroyed tries to pretend that it does not really matter, etc.

4 In groups of three or four. Workmen have painted a park bench. They have gone off to find the 'wet paint' notice. While they are away two people come along and sit on the bench to eat their lunch. When the workmen return with the notice, what happens? Again, the adult can help the children develop the scene by being, for example, the foreman who comes along in order to try to sort things out. This role-play scene can be either realistic or more fantastic. For example, it may simply be based on the reactions of the couple to their ruined clothing, or humour may be explored in the ways in which the workmen try to remove the people from the bench to which they have stuck.

5 In groups. Children playing with a ball kick it into the garden of another house. Who owns the house? What kind of people are they? Do the children decide, on the basis of the kind of people who live in the house, to leave the ball; to sneak in and try to get it back; to go to the door and ask for it, etc.? What happens when they carry out the actions decided on? How do they explain the situation to their parents in a subsequent lesson situation? Again it may be necessary for the adult to take a role or to suggest various possibilities for the children to act out.

IMPROVISATION

Like the more advanced forms of role-play, improvisation gives children an opportunity both to act out and rehearse the appropriate behaviour for real social situations, and to engage in more imaginative situations involving roles which they may never be expected to encounter in reality. Improvisation tends to be linked to dialogue, and, as this dialogue is developed spontaneously by the children in the course of the work, improvisation demands a fair degree of linguistic ability. The one exception to this is the type of improvisation in which music, or some other stimulus, is used to provide an atmosphere or mood and the children act out in movement or mime the scene suggested by the stimulus. This latter form of improvisation is much simpler than the former, but it still demands a high degree of concentration from pupils, the ability to express themselves in movement, and the self-discipline to work co-operatively as members of a group.

Improvisation of Social Situations

Mentally handicapped children may not fully understand the difference between behaviour which is appropriate in a supermarket or self-service store or restaurant, and the different behaviour which is necessary in a shop or restaurant where they are served. Improvised scenes set in each of these situations can help children understand the different forms of behaviour necessary in each.

1   Half the children are employed in a supermarket: some are at the checkout, some are stacking shelves or pricing tins; while the rest are customers loading their trolleys and paying for their goods. An element of excitement may be added if one customer finds that she has lost her purse or has insufficient money to pay for goods or is in a great hurry and tries to persuade other customers to let her go to the checkout first, etc.

2   Contrast this with the scene in a fruit shop in which customers have to wait to be served and cannot test the quality of fruit or weigh their own goods.

3   In groups of four. One child is the assistant in a shoe shop. One is at the checkout of the self-service shoe store next door. The other two children are customers. Each tries both shops before finding the goods they want. Encourage the children to talk about the differences in behaviour which they portrayed in their acting out.

4   In groups. One child is a waitress, and the others are customers in a restaurant, ordering and eating a meal. Either act out the scene quite realistically, or introduce elements such as the waitress being rushed, soup getting spilt, no salt on the table, etc. Contrast with a scene set in a busy self-service restaurant.

5   In groups. A mother wakes up one morning with 'flu. Her husband has to phone the doctor. Other pupils act as the receptionist, doctor and, perhaps, a chemist. This, and similar situations, can give children practice in making simulated telephone conversations.

A useful variation is to pre-record a message on a tape-recorder and to set the tape-recorder up as the doctor's answering machine. On an appropriate signal from the tape, the children leave their message for the doctor.

As a follow up, and to give the chilren practice in using speech to convey precise information, the tape-recorder can be used in a similar way as the basis of a game. A child records a 'secret' message on the tape. It can be as simple as his name, or as complex as the child can make it. The teacher and other children have to listen and say what the message is. The quicker the message is guessed, the better the messenger has been in sharing his secret. This is particularly helpful as a way of encouraging clarity of speech among pupils who have articulatory difficulties. As a variation, the adult can pre-record secret instructions which the group have to carry out in order, for example, to find a hidden treasure (a sweet or some other item which the adult has previously hidden). This helps children respond to precise verbal information.

Less Realistic Situations

As a contrast to improvisations involving social situations, children may be encouraged to act out imaginative scenes or scenes involving a much larger group of characters.

1 To a suitable piece of music, such as 'Neptune' from *The Planets Suite* by Holst, the children are deep sea divers trying to raise a treasure from a sunken ship. All the movements must be in slow motion.

2 A group of people are having a picnic on a quiet beach. The weather changes and it starts to thunder. They seek shelter in a nearby cave. What happens next? Encourage the children to make suggestions and to try them out.

3 The scene is a busy airport. Some children are holidaymakers, arriving with luggage, checking in, checking tickets, buying sweets or magazines for the journey, etc. Others are serving in the shop or buffet, officiating at the check-in desk, etc. One child may be responsible for making flight announcements. Others may be cleaners or mechanics, preparing the plane for take-off. In a group situation of this kind it is generally necessary to prepare the children for working individually within a group by discussing in advance what is likely to be involved in the scene, and by giving the children practice in the individual elements before combining these within a group scene.

4 It is early in the morning. One by one passengers arrive at the bus stop to catch a bus for work, or shopping, or some other reason. As the bus does not arrive on time

the passengers begin to express their impatience and to discuss with each other why the bus may be late and why it matters to them.

5   A group of people get up one morning to discover that a plant in a neighbour's garden has grown enormously tall in the night. They discuss why this is so, and what to do about it.

EXTENSIONS OF IMPROVISATION AND ROLE-PLAY

Both improvisation and role-play can help children increase and extend their understanding and use of language. As a follow-up to these activities, and as a means of consolidating the new vocabulary introduced, I often encourage children to make up a group poem using the sounds and words they have worked on in their scenes. No single child need contribute more than one word or phrase. Each suggestion is noted by the adult and put together in an appropriate way to make the 'poem', the words of which will all be those given by the children, with only the odd linking word added by the adult. When the order has been decided on, the children each say only one or two lines, or make appropriate sounds – either vocally or with a percussion instrument, and these are then tape-recorded. Often, these simple poems can be very effective, and children are generally very proud of having made them up. Try to accept every contribution, even if it is only a single sound, such as the sound of the wind or the sea. Children also enjoy making a collage to illustrate their poem, which can then be displayed on the wall. Even though the children may not be able to read the words, they will know what the poem is about, and they know that it is theirs.

Here are some examples of the kind of thing I mean. These poems were all produced by mildly handicapped pupils under the age of twelve. Not all the pupils were linguistically competent, but all had a fair level of comprehension of speech and could make sounds. The first two were developed by a group of nine year-olds who had been working on improvisations with a sea theme. The third was made up by a group of older boys who had worked on an improvisation based on exploring a jungle.

Sea

Sea. Sssss
Waves. Ssssss
Waves splashing.
Shsh . . .shsh . . .
Donkey rides and ice-cream cones.
Clip, clop, clip, clop,
Hooves on stones.

Storm at Sea

Sh . . . Sh . . .
Angry waves.
The wind blows the waves into curling circles.
The heavy sea carries the ship on to the rocks.
Whoooooooo . . . sh . . .
Shipwreck!
The mast cracks.
Help! Help! Ahoy there!
The lifeboat hurries to the rescue.
Help! Help! Ahoy there!
And every life is saved.

Mud

Mud, mud, mud,
Squelch!
Mud.
Mud on feet.
Mud.
Sssssssss . . . eeeeee
A bird flies up and squawks.
Crack! What's that?
Ssssss . . . snakes!

Rattle, rattle, rattle, rattlesnakes!
No! Ssssssssticks.
Ahhhhh.

(Throughout the entire poem, one group kept repeating the words mud and slime at various intervals and with varying degrees of loudness and speed.)

THE USE OF THE TAPE-RECORDER IN IMPROVISATION

I have already given a couple of examples of where a tape-recorder can be useful as a stimulus or follow up in improvised work. But there are a number of other ways in which a tape-recorder can be an invaluable piece of equipment within the drama lesson. For example, for the jungle improvisation which led them to the above poem, the boys spent a number of lessons in preparing a tape which would provide a background for their improvised speech and movement. We discussed and decided on the kinds of sounds likely to be heard in a jungle and experimented with different ways of making sounds to produce the background effects we wanted. Various types of whistle produced bird song. Different kinds of crisp and soft paper, rustled and crushed in the hand close to the microphone, produced the effect of different types of terrain being trampled on. A pencil pulled sharply across the rough side of a ruler gave a very good rattlesnake effect, while finger clicking, hand clapping and soft blowing gave the effect of a forest fire. The boys enjoyed making the tape for its own sake, but the fact that it was going to be used as an integral part of their improvised drama gave it a focus and purpose which meant that the boys tried hard to find inventive solutions that would give the exact effect they wanted for their drama.

With a younger or less able group, the adult can provide a stimulus for improvisation by pre-recording a series of sound effects on tape and asking the children to suggest what the sounds represent and where the scene might take place. This leads on to a discussion of who might be making the sounds, what was happening at the time, and what might happen afterwards. Once the children have agreed on the setting, the characters and the actions suggested to them by the tape, the tape itself becomes the background to their improvisation. Often this will be completely different from the sequence which was in the adult's mind when she made the tape. I once prepared a tape which I thought was fairly representative of fairground noises and effects; the pupils, however, interpreted the sounds as the noise of a musical box and a factory and ended up by doing an improvised scene in which they were workers in a factory which made musical boxes. The fact that children may interpret a tape in a different way from that envisaged, however, is unimportant. What is important, and where the value of this form of work lies, is in the fact that children are listening to sounds, taking an interest in sound production, and using sounds as a means of extending and exercising their imaginations.

OTHER STIMULUS MATERIALS

Let me finish off this chapter on role-play and improvisation by suggesting just a few of the other stimulus materials which may be useful in developing this form of work. Records have already been mentioned as a means of creating an atmosphere or rhythm for a piece of work. The other advantage of using music in this way is that it can create a control mechanism which is linked to the drama work and is not imposed externally upon the work. The children can be encouraged to 'freeze' when the music stops, thus enabling the adult to feed in extra information or call the group together for discussion. Changes in the tempo or volume of the music, as well as natural breaks in the music, can all act as signals for a change in the dramatic action. For example, in the deep sea diver improvisation referred to earlier, a sudden surge in the music can provide a signal which suggests to the children that a diver has lost his mask, the cargo of the ship has suddenly shifted, a shark is approaching, etc. Incidents such as these can expand and extend simple themes, and, simply by fading or increasing the volume of the music, the adult is in a very good position to ensure that the work remains organised and productive.

Everyday objects, or unusual objects, can also provide a lead in to improvised work. A collection of sea shells provides a simple and effective lead in to improvisations based on the beach or sea. An item of clothing can be used as a means of establishing role-play based on the character whom the children think would be likely to own and wear such an item. An unusual and attractive empty box can lead on to speculation about what was in the box, where it was found, who owned it, and why it is now empty. Again, the suggestions given can form the basis of improvisation or role-play. A piece of paper made to look like an old map of an island with a cross in the centre, can provide a natural and easy way of acting out a scene involving either the finding of pirate's treasure, the encampment of shipwrecked sailors, or the planning by robbers of where to plant their 'loot' and its subsequent discovery by the police, etc.

Another stimulus technique used by many drama teachers is that of using 'odd' people as a means of introducing improvisation. This technique involves gaining the co-operation of at least one other adult who will dress for the part and be 'discovered' by the children. This adult remains in role throughout, while the other adult acts with the children, making suggestions and helping them to decide on and act out ways of dealing with the intruder. For example, the colleague may become a sleeping tramp in one corner of a classroom. The children have to decide whether he is friendly or not, whether they should move him or tell him to go away, how they should react to him, and so on. Other possibilities include: a sad clown whom the children must try to cheer up; a lost dog which may, or may not, be friendly; a spaceman who has appeared on earth – is he one of ours, or does he come from space? How might they find out?

If sufficient resources are available it is also possible to develop improvised drama into a whole-school or class project, in which all the other school work is performed as part of the dramatic situation. This technique requires a great deal of preplanning, but it can have effective results in terms of learning and recall. A headmaster of a special school in Yorkshire, for example, involved the whole school, including teachers, parents, dinner ladies and the caretaker, in a project which was based on finding Bluebeard and acquiring his secret hoard of treasure. All the reading, counting, art-work and writing was linked to the general dramatic action, with the children having to decode secret messages left by the teacher, to count out the number of steps required to find the next message, or to write instructions or descriptive accounts of where items were to be found.

I used a similar approach when, on one occasion, the classroom was transformed for a few days into a garden fête, complete with stalls and sideshows. All the work, which was carried out with the help and co-operation of the head teacher and the class teacher, centred around the activities of the fête. The children decided on the type of stalls, decorated them, prepared the notices, made up games of skill, etc. When the fête was ready, one child declared it open and another class, who had been invited to attend and had been provided with cardboard money, came in and became the customers for the various stalls and sideshows presided over by the children.

Exercises such as these tend to be more useful, however, with children who are developmentally fairly mature, and who have fairly good linguistic ability. Such exercises can provide a useful basis for learning and consolidating skills, but these isolated instances of 'special' drama demand a great deal of organisation and preparation to set them up, not to mention having to cope with the general excitement generated by them. These special occasions may provide peak experiences which will encourage a flow of conversation both during and after the event. It is unlikely, however, that such forms of drama would be used frequently in any one school year. And the simpler forms of stimuli such as percussion, visits, outings, tapes, records, toys and objects, or even a picture brought in by one of the children, are likely to provide the basis for the regular, on-going work which makes up the normal, classroom drama.

11 Three Graded Themes

Earlier in the book I suggested that basing lessons on a theme makes it relatively easy to plan a series of lessons. In Chapter Six we looked at how the theme of something as familiar as a ball could be developed and could diversify in a number of different directions, depending on the age, interests or ability of the children. In this chapter I have taken three of the ideas suggested in Chapter Six and show the different material which was used in the actual lessons based on these themes.

The first theme, Christmas, is the simplest of the three, and can be used with younger children or with children who have only limited imaginative ability. But I have included a short Christmas Play which the more able child might be able to tackle. The second theme is 'shape', and in this one I try to show how drama work can link with other areas of work in the development of simple mathematical concepts. The last theme is the most complex, and is more suitable for children who have had practice in drama, or who have relatively good imaginative ability. The theme of this one is 'circus'. As we have already looked at the kind of movement and dramatic play which might be included in this theme, the material given here is mainly the stories and rhymes which can be used to supplement the movement and dramatic play.

THEME 1: CHRISTMAS

Mime and Movement

1   *In pairs* cut down Christmas trees with a two-handed saw. Use any lively, rhythmic music as an accompaniment. I often use the pop song *Popcorn*.*

2   *Working together as a group* lift the felled trees and pass them down to each other. The last child loads them on to the lorry. Again, the same music makes a suitable accompaniment.

3   *Working together as a group* unload the trees from the lorry and stack them outside shops for the people to buy (same music).

4   *In pairs*, one is a shopkeeper, the other is buying a tree.

Dramatic Play

1   *Working in unison* each child is one of Santa's helpers. Each is making a toy for a child at Christmas. Having discussed the kind of toys they might be making, allow the children to practise, in unison, the kind of movements involved: hammering, sawing, painting, gluing, cutting, stitching, etc. When the children have practised the various movements, allow them to choose one particular toy and each makes his or her own toy. When the toy is finished it is loaded into Santa's sack. (To the music of *La Boutique Fantasque* by Respighi.)

2   *Working in unison*, be different kinds of toys in the toy shop: bouncing like balls (single taps on a drum or tambour); marching like soldiers (marching rhythm tapped out); different kinds of dolls and soft toys (walking dolls that say 'mama', Paddington Bears eating marmalade sandwiches, floppy dolls, or dancing dolls); being radio controlled toy cars/fire-engines/police cars (the children supply sounds themselves).

*For details of the music suggested see Bibliography

3   *Individual work within a group.* Exercise two, above, ma
    be developed into a version of the magic toyshop, i
    which all the toys begin to move, etc. on a given signal
    and on another signal go back to being static. Again *L
    Boutique Fantasque* or Delibes' *Coppelia* will provid
    suitable background music.

4   *Working in unison,* each child becomes Santa, packing
    his sack with toys; creeping into houses; checking t
    make sure everyone is asleep; quietly filling stocking
    and placing parcels under trees; finally riding off and
    giving his reindeer a bucket of water to drink. (*Morning
    Mood* from the *Peer Gynt Suite* makes a suitable
    accompaniment.)

5   *Working individually within a group,* each child is asleep
    On a given signal each child awakes and begins to
    unwrap parcels and open presents in his stocking. The
    children have to show, by what they do with them
    what the toys are that they have received.

6   *Working together in a group,* lift down a big box of fragile
    Christmas tree decorations and unpack them carefully.
    All help to decorate an enormous Christmas tree.

Speech and Action Rhymes

1   There's a stocking on the wall by the clock.
    There's a stocking on the wall, and a sock.
    We'll creep upstairs so softly,
    We won't make any noise,
    And Santa Claus will come
    And fill our stockings
    Full of toys.
    We wake up in the morning
    And rush downstairs
    To see
    Stockings filled with presents
    Beneath the Christmas tree.

2   Santa brought a present
    A present just for me.
    If I open up my present
    I wonder what I'll see?

(With the least able children it may be necessary to use a
pillow case and some real, unwrapped presents. Take each
item out very slowly and encourage the children to guess
what it is. When each item is guessed ask the children to
mime what they would do with it.)

Stories to Dramatise

1   The Bird Stocking

It was Christmas day. Outside the house it was very cold
and everything was covered with thick, white snow. But
inside the house, where it was bright and warm, John and
Margaret were busy unwrapping their Christmas
presents.

'Oh, look,' said John. 'I've got a fire-engine. That's just
what I wanted.'

'And I've got a spaceman. That's what I wanted,' said
Margaret, happily.

They unwrapped all the presents, books, and sweets,
and toys, and, and . . .

'Daddy!' said Margaret, 'what's this?' And she held up a
sort of red stocking thing that was full of nuts and seeds.

'I've got one too,' said John. 'What is it, Daddy?'

Daddy smiled. 'It's a funny sort of present,' he said, 'but
I think you'll like it. Come with me.'

Daddy led them to the back door.

'Wrap up warm and put on your boots. We're going out
into the garden.'

'But why, Daddy?' asked John.

'Wait and see,' said his father, and he opened the back
door and walked out into the cold, snow-filled garden.
Then he did a very funny thing. He took John's stocking

thing, and Margaret's stocking thing, and he tied them both on to a branch of a tree in the garden.

'There,' he said. 'Now we go inside and wait.'

Wait? Wait for what? And why had Daddy tied the presents on to a tree in the garden? It was all very strange. And John and Margaret didn't understand it at all. Then Daddy said, 'Sh . . . very quiet. Here they come. Look out of the window.'

John and Margaret looked out of the window, and they saw lots of birds. Little blue and yellow birds, brown birds, and even one with a red breast – a robin. And the birds were all perched on the branch of the tree trying to peck at the stocking things.

'Oh, I know what our presents are now,' said Margaret. 'They're Christmas stockings. From Santa Claus. For the birds.'

'Yes,' said Daddy, 'and I'm sure the birds will come to the garden every day now until the cold weather goes away.'

'Oh, I hope so,' said Margaret.

'Yes,' said John. 'I like my fire-engine. But I think my bird-stocking was the best present of all.'

And I do too. Don't you?

(This story is suitable for dramatisation by virtually any of the methods described earlier, except the open-ended approach. I generally use a real 'bird-stocking' as a visual aid, and follow up the story by allowing the children to hang it on a suitable place out of doors, but within sight of a window from which they can watch the birds feeding. A bird tree can also be made by tying pieces of bacon rind, nuts, etc., on to a twiggy branch, which can be placed outside or on a window ledge.)

2   *The Nativity* (written in the form of a script)
(*A group of children carry cardboard stars covered in kitchen foil. They walk over and sit in a corner of the room on a bench. They hold their stars up in front of them. They sing* Away in a

Manger. *When they reach the line,* the stars in the bright sky, *they hold their stars very high. Mary and Joseph come in, Mary carrying the baby. One child with a star leads them to another corner of the room. Joseph pretends to knock on a door. A child mimes opening the door.)*

MARY: Have you a room please?

LADY: No. No room. *(She mimes closing door and goes away to sit down. Mary and Joseph move a few paces forward and repeat the same sequence with another child. This may be repeated a few times. Until . . .)*

MARY: Have you a room, please?

LADY: Come with me. Will this do? *(She points to area beside the stars' bench)*

MARY: Thank you.

JOSEPH: Thank you.

(Mary and Joseph sit on floor and Mary places the baby in a cradle and fusses over it. Landladies stand beside the stars. Stars sing and point with stars to the shepherds who come in during the song and kneel before the baby. Again, a child with a star leads them in. The melody of the song is given on p. 202.)

VERSE 1:   See the shepherds coming, coming,
            Coming from afar.
            To see the baby Jesus
            And following a star.

CHORUS: Baby Jesus born today
            Baby Jesus born today
            See the shepherds coming, coming,
            Coming from afar.

(During the chorus, the landladies can add a percussion accompaniment to the stars' song. During the next verse, the stars point to the Kings, who are led in by a star. They come to the baby, bow, present their gifts, and kneel at the side.)

VERSE 2:   The wise men came to see the baby
            Lying in the hay
            The wise men came and gave the baby
            Birthday gifts that day.

CHORUS: Baby Jesus born today
          Baby Jesus born today
          The wise men came to see the baby
          Lying in the hay.

(During the final verse, the landladies and stars come forward and give their gifts and then go back to stand behind the others. If possible, add a jingle bell or chime bar accompaniment to this verse.)

VERSE 3: All the stars were shining and the
          Bells rang out so gay
          And all the world was full of joy
          On that first Christmas day.

CHORUS: Baby Jesus born today.
          Baby Jesus born today.
          All the world was full of joy
          On that first Christmas day. *(repeat last two lines)*

Play: The Christmas Stars

As this play is considerably more complex than the preceding one, it is likely that only the more advanced pupils will be able to tackle it. It is particularly useful, however, with a group of pupils of mixed ability as there are possibilities in it for both verbal and non-verbal parts and for some considerable degree of music and percussion work.

(The children are standing around with dusters in one hand. In the other hand, a cardboard star covered in tinfoil, dull side out. A small child has star covered in tinfoil, shiny side out and sprinkled with glitter. Throughout the following dialogue she is busy polishing her star.)

STAR 1:   I'm fed up.
STAR 2:   So am I.
STAR 3:   I'm tired of polishing these stars.
STAR 4:   *(yawning)* I'm just tired.

STAR 5:	No one ever looks up in the sky at the stars now.
STAR 6	I don't care if nobody sees my star.
STAR 1:	Nobody will. It's all dull and dirty.
STAR 6:	It is not.
STAR 1:	Yes it is.
STAR 6:	It's not as bad as yours! Look at it.

(Other stars look at Star 1's dull star and laugh)

STAR 2:	*(pointing to little star)* Look at her star.
STAR 1:	Well, she's new.
STAR 6:	She'll soon get tired of polishing.

(Enter starkeeper like sergeant major)

| STARKEEPER: | Attention! Star children, stand by your stars. |

(Children stand to attention and show their stars. He moves along as if on parade inspecting the troops.)

STARKEEPER:	Oh dear! Oh dear! These stars are so dull. Ttt! And we have an important job to do.
STAR 1:	A job?
OTHER STARS:	What is it?
STARKEEPER:	Do you see these two people over there? *(enter Mary and Joseph as if exhausted. They take a few steps and Mary stumbles as if about to fall.)* They are on their way to Bethlehem. Tomorrow night the baby Jesus, the Son of God, will be born in Bethlehem.
STARS:	Oh!
STARKEEPER:	Watch. *(Mary and Joseph knock on door and the lady opens it (mime).)*
JOSEPH:	Do you have a room? ⎫
LADY:	No, I'm sorry. No room. ⎬ repeat three times
JOSEPH:	Do you have a room? ⎭
MAN:	No, but I can let you sleep in the stable.

(Man leads Mary and Joseph to stable where they sit and fall asleep.)

| STARKEEPER: | We need a star to guide the Wise Men and |

the Shepherds to the baby Jesus. Polish
your stars, star children. I'll come back
later.

(Exit while stars polish furiously. He re-enters).

STARKEEPER: ATTENTION! *(he inspects the stars.)* Oh
dear! Oh dear! It's no use. The stars are
still too dull.

STAR 1:   *(pointing to the little star)* What about her?

STAR 2:   She's too small!

STAR 4:   But she's bright.

STARKEEPER: Sh! Look! The baby Jesus has been born.
*(Sound of bells and Mary mimes placing a
baby in the cradle. Joseph stands beside her.
Shepherds enter and sit as if half asleep.)*

STARKEEPER: Little star, *you* must guide the Wise Men
and the Shepherds. Can you do it?

LITTLE STAR: I'll try.

OTHER STARS: Good luck!

STAR 1:   And we will sing to help you on your
way.

(Stars sing softly the first verse of the song.)

Shepherds they are coming, coming
Coming from afar
To see the baby Jesus
And following a star.

(The little star moves forward and beckons to the shepherds.)

SHEPHERD 1:   Look at that bright star.

SHEPHERD 2:   Listen to the angels singing.

SHEPHERD 3:   What are they saying?

(Stars sing first chorus.

Baby Jesus born today
Baby Jesus born today
See the shepherds coming
Coming from afar.)

SHEPHERD: Baby Jesus born today! Come my friends
let us follow the star.

*(Stars repeat the verse and chorus and shepherds follow star to
where Mary, Joseph and the baby are. They kneel. Little star goes*

*and beckons to the wise men. They come in and follow the star to
the manger. During this the other stars sing.)*

Verse 2:   The Wise Men came to see the baby
                        Lying in the hay
                        The Wise Men came and gave the baby
                        Birthday gifts that day

Chorus: Baby Jesus born today
                        Baby Jesus born today
                        The Wise Men came to see the baby
                        Lying in the hay.

KING 1:   Gold for the baby Jesus.
KING 2:   Frankincense I bring.
KING 3:   Myrrh for the Son of God.

(All three kneel and present gifts. All sing Away in a Manger.
*As they do so the stars move round to stand behind Mary and
Joseph and hold up their stars. The little star stands to one side, a
star in one hand, and a small pocket torch in the other. She lights
up her star with the torch.)*

VOICE: And so was born in Bethlehem the baby
                        Jesus, the Son of God.

*(All sing. People who were landladies enter with bells and
marakas and stand beside the others.)*

Verse 3:   The little stars were shining
                        And the bells rang out so gay
                        And all the world was full of joy
                        On that first Christmas Day.

Chorus: Baby Jesus born today
                        Baby Jesus born today
                        And all the world was full of joy
                        On that first Christmas Day.

See The Shepherds Coming

KEY: G MAJOR

Additional source material can be found in *The Christmas Book* edited by James Reeves and published by Heinemann, 1968. See also *Mrs Pepperpot's Christmas* by Alf Proysen, published by Puffin Books, 1981

THEME 2: SHAPE

Mime and movement

1 To establish the concept of 'straightness', move quickly over the floor in straight lines, following a leader. On a given signal, change direction, but still move in a straight line.

2 Make body into a long, thin, straight shape,
   a on a drum-beat stretch up as tall and thin and straight as possible, then, on cymbal beat, flop slowly to the ground;

b repeat the exercise moving out sideways with arms straight.

3 Pretend to throw a ball in straight lines to knock down skittles in a bowling alley;

4 Pretend to be men painting the straight white/yellow lines on the road – this can be done to suitable music and can form part of a simple acting out sequence in which the children are motorists being redirected away from driving over the newly painted straight lines;

5 Contrast 'straight' with 'curved' or 'wavy'. Play follow-the-leader all over the room. Try to cover as much floor space as possible, twisting and weaving in all directions to make curved or wavy paths over the floor. This exercise can be great fun if done out of doors after a fresh fall of snow, as the children can see the paths they make. It is also possible for the children to see the straight or curved paths they make, if the floor is covered in newsprint and children dip their feet in finger paint. Not all children will enjoy this, however, as some children have an aversion to becoming 'dirty'.

6 Move around the room in curved lines, weaving in and out of each other. The object is to try and be as wavy as possible without touching anyone else. The same exercise can become a pretend game of 'dodgems' – the children being dodgem-cars at a fair.

7 Follow up the movement work with art work in which the children experiment with the different kinds of lines that can be made on paper with string, sticks, or other objects dipped in paint.

Circles
1 The same follow-my-leader as before, but moving in circles of different sizes.
2 Make circles in the air with hands, feet, elbows, noses, etc.
3 Pretend to paint the sun in the sky.

Story: The Circle
Once there was a big, round circle.
It became very tired being just a circle – so
It became a big, round, striped ball.
The ball bounced up and down, up and down, up and
down – then
Splash!
It landed in the middle of a big round puddle.
The ball didn't like being wet – so
It turned into a balloon.
The balloon floated up, up, up to the sky – then
It saw something else that was big and round.
It was the sun.
A big, round, yellow sun.
But the sun was very hot.
And the balloon didn't like being hot – so
It floated down to the ground
And became a penny.
A round shiny penny.
John saw the penny.
He picked it up.
He took it to the shop.
He bought a penny lollipop.
A round, red lollipop.
He ate it all up.
And that was the end of that!

Dramatise by the narrative method, encouraging the
children to act out, in unison, being first the ball and then
the balloon. Act out feeling the heat of the sun on the face
and becoming hot; splashing in puddles and walking all
round them. Devise a scene in which one group is the sun,
moving round and round. The others are clouds which
move in front of the sun and turn into raindrops which
drop down to become a round puddle. Alternate different
percussion instruments for the sun and the rain. Using
cardboard or real pennies, role-play the finding of the
penny, the buying and eating of the lollipop.

Speech and Action Rhymes

1   Stand up straight.
    As straight as you can.
    Arms by your side
    Like a soldier man.

    Left, right, left, right
    Marching in a row.
    Left, right, left right,
    On we go.

2   The snake in the grass
    Slithers and slips and slides along.
    S . . . . . . ssss
    Hissssssing.

3   Make yourself as tall as a house,
    Up, up up – so high.
    Make yourself as small as a mouse,
    Down, down, in the grass you lie,
    Curled up small.
    A round, furry ball.

Link all the movement, speech and drama work to experience of real objects and their shapes. For example, collect as many straight-sided objects as possible. Beside them, place a collection of objects with curved or indefinable shapes, such as lumps of plasticine, oddly shaped bean bags, bits of twisted metal or pipe cleaners, etc. Beside them place all the round objects the children can find, and encourage the children to identify the different shapes they see in the piles. Then remove a few objects and try to get the children to sort them out again on the basis of their shape, giving help where necessary.*

*The *Starters* series of books published by Macdonald are a useful source of background material for this theme

THEME 3: THE CIRCUS

A number of the activities which may be used in developing this theme have already been given some detailed consideration in Chapter Six. The material given here is additional material which may be used in expanding the theme and developing it further in more advanced dramatic activities.

Circus Rhymes

Come to the circus. The circus is in town.
Come to the circus and see the funny clowns.
Red noses, baggy pants – Look! They're falling down!
Come to the circus. The circus is in town.

Elephants. Elephants.
Swinging tails and swinging trunks.
Acrobats. Acrobats.
Jumping forward, jumping back.
Horses dressed in silver, prancing round and round.
Come to the circus. The circus is in town.

A seal in the circus we found.
Turning a ball round and round.
Now why, do you suppose,
That seal, with his nose
Is turning a ball round and round?

The lion tamer took his stick and waved it in the air.
The mighty lion gave a growl and jumped from here to there.
The lion tamer shouted, 'Hup!'
The lion gave a roar.
The lion tamer shouted, 'Help!'
And ran right out the door!

A Simple Mime Play Based on the Theme

RINGMASTER: (*spoken by teacher*) Ladies and gentlemen, we proudly present
'The (*name of school or town*) Circus'.

(To the music of 76 Trombones, *children move around being the various characters in the circus parade.)*

RINGMASTER: The clowns!

(To the honky-tonk piano music of Winifred Atwell, the clowns step into the middle, chase each other, fall down, trip, bounce up and down, etc.)

RINGMASTER: The jugglers!

(To the music of The Sting, *jugglers step into the middle and mime juggling with balls or clubs, spinning plates, etc.)*

RINGMASTER: The lion tamer!

(To Pink Floyd's Just Another Brick in the Wall, *one child is the lion tamer, the other the lion. At the end of the act the tables are turned and the lion tamer is chased by the lion.)*

RINGMASTER: The tightrope walkers!

(To Leroy Anderson's The Waltzing Cat – *tightrope walkers do all the appropriate actions – putting one foot in front of the other, waving slightly to regain balance, holding up an umbrella to keep balance, etc.)*

RINGMASTER: The Grand Parade!

(Repeat the walk around led by the Ringmaster who pretends to beat on a drum. Use the same music as for the opening sequence. Add any other acts you may feel the children would enjoy and could do.)

Story to Dramatise

Joey

Once there was a clown called Joey. He worked in the circus. Joey wasn't a very good clown. He couldn't make anyone laugh. Now, a clown who can't make anyone laugh is no good in the circus. So, one day the circus master called Joey and told him he would have to leave the circus.

That afternoon when all the other clowns were getting ready to go into the circus ring, Joey just picked up his make-up, his red nose, and his baggy trousers, and wandered off down the road to sit by the river and wonder what to do.

Joey heard a noise. Woof. Woof, woof. It was a little black dog. It had no collar and no lead. It didn't belong to anyone. It was just a little stray dog.

'Go away,' said Joey, crossly. 'Go away. I don't want you.' But the little dog didn't go away. It just lay there, looking at Joey.

Joey took out his mouth organ and began to play a little tune to cheer himself up. And the little dog stood up on its two back legs and began to dance. Yes. Really. It danced round and round in time to Joey's music. It looked so funny that Joey had to stop playing his mouth organ because he was laughing so much.

Then Joey had an idea. (*Stop the story here if using open-ended approach to dramatisation.*)

'Come on, dog,' he called, and began to run all the way back to the circus.

He was just in time. The clowns were just about to go into the circus ring. Joey ran in behind them.

'Come on, dog,' he shouted, as he began to play his mouth organ.

The little black dog stood up on its hind legs in the middle of the circus ring. And it began to dance. After a minute, a little boy began to laugh. Then another, and another, and another! All the people began to laugh and to clap.

'Bravo, bravo,' they shouted.

The circus master came into the ring to see what all the noise was about. When he saw Joey and the little black dog, he began to laugh too.

'Do I get my job back, then?' asked Joey.

'Yes,' said the circus master.

'Woof,' said the little black dog.

And all the people laughed.

Good sources of background material are:

Circuses by Allen James, published by Oxford University Press, 1978, and *Circus* by E. Cooper, published by Macdonald Educational, 1979.

12   Playmaking and Performance

Many handicapped children will have no need to show their drama work. For them, simply taking part in drama will be an enjoyable learning experience and they would gain little from having to show their work off to anyone. Some children, too, may not have reached the stage at which they understand what it means to 'perform'. For these children also there will be no need to show their work.

But there may be a number of children who could benefit from showing their work to a small audience of other children, parents or teachers. The benefits which such children may derive from performing their work in front of others are a sense of self-worth and pride in their achievements. These are just as necessary for the handicapped child as they are for other children. So, if the children show that they would like to perform their work for others, and if you think they would benefit from doing so, there is no reason why they should not put on a play, a sequence of movement or a concert for others to enjoy.

With young children, and with handicapped children, it is unlikely that you would ever approach this type of work by producing a script and asking them to learn the words. Playmaking, for young or handicapped children, is much more likely to grow out of the normal work done in the course of the drama lesson. For example, if the children have been dramatising a story and have enjoyed it particularly, they may want to repeat it and develop it further. Such dramatisation can often form the basis of a simple performance in which the children use the words they have mastered in the course of their class work and carry out the sequence of actions devised in class. The simple addition of a few items of costume or one or two props can turn a classroom dramatisation of this kind into a play which can be performed for others. Similarly, if children have been working on a sequence of music and movement, or group improvisation activities, these may also form the basis for a simple performance.

I do feel, however, that it is necessary to ensure that the audience is one which will understand and accept the children's play in the spirit in which it is presented. In other words, the audience will be prepared for a spontaneous performance which has grown out of the children's normal class work, rather than expecting a staged show in the conventional sense.

When putting on any kind of play with mentally handicapped children. I prefer not to use a stage, even in schools where there is one available. There are two reasons for this. First, many children naturally tend to work 'in the round', and it can be difficult for them to adopt the rather unnatural movements that are required on a stage in order that the actors can face the audience. But if children simply perform their play in the middle of a hall or in a classroom, there is no need to ask them to face in any particular direction and they will, naturally, turn to face the people to whom they are talking in the play. Secondly, some children may be un-nerved by the unfamiliar experience of acting on a stage, and may be happier to act out their work in the familiar environment in which it was developed and rehearsed. It can, however, lend atmosphere to the performance and give the children a sense of 'occasion' if it is possible to import a couple of coloured spots and provide some background music in keeping with the theme being presented.

If you do decide to tackle a performance with your classes, be prepared for the unexpected. The children may not do the same things as they did on previous occasions.

They may change the words, the actions, or even the plot of the play as it goes along. I vividly remember one occasion when an audio-visual team from a local college of education was coming to film the work of one group of children who had been working on the Christmas story. The film was to be used as demonstration material for student teachers. The performance given by the children was one on which they had been working for a number of weeks, using their own words and developing the actions in class. On previous occasions, in rehearsal, when Mary had sunk down into the hay of the stable, exhausted after her journey, Joseph had asked her if she would like a cup of tea, and Mary had accepted this with thanks. On the day of the filming, however, Mary decided to change her lines. When asked if she would like some tea, she replied in a very plaintive voice, 'I'd rather have a whisky.' Needless to say, the film crew left it in.

On another occasion a whole class was to present a short, mimed sequence as part of the entertainment at a parents' evening. There was no dialogue, but the children had to make various background noises as part of the dramatic action. At one point in the story, a robber creeps into a wood to hide the gold he has stolen, and, when he leaves, the birds swoop down and carry it back to the owner. The child who was to play the robber was the most gregarious child in the class and, in class work, was always the first to volunteer to take a leading part. On the night of the show, however, he took fright and point blank refused to go on. As his part was obviously crucial to the play it did not look as if we were going to be able to present the item. In the end, one of the staff substituted for him and became the robber. He was quite happy to go on as one of the birds along with the other children.

The first example demonstrates the kind of amusing and perfectly harmless incident which can occur when children show their improvised work. The second, however, demonstrates a rather more harmful aspect of this form of performance. As it happened, the child was happy to go on as one of the birds, and seemed to enjoy both doing so and the applause of the audience at the end. But the fact that he had opted out of his original part could have led to an awkward situation in which the other children blamed him for letting them down. As the whole point of this work is to enhance the child's self-esteem and to encourage co-operation, such a situation could have back fired.

In deciding to put on any kind of show, therefore, it is important to be prepared for this kind of thing to happen, and to plan the work in such a way that the children do not feel they are being put under any pressure. This particular incident was a salutary lesson for me, and one which I have never forgotten. I have tried not to repeat it by making sure that all the children are sufficiently familiar with the work, and have had the opportunity to practise a range of parts in classroom rehearsals before attempting to show the work. Under these circumstances, if a child wishes to opt out, or change his part at the last moment, there is no harm done and it will simply be like another class drama situation in which the children take whichever part is assigned to them on that particular day. If items of clothing and props are kept to the minimum necessary to give the 'feel' of the play, there should be few problems if parts have to be changed at the last moment.

In order to give some idea of the range of work which may be tackled by mentally handicapped children I have included four plays: *The King Who couldn't stop Sneezing*, *Michael's Midnight Adventure*, *King George and the Dragon*, and *The Three Little Pigs*. All of these were developed out of ordinary class work and, as far as possible, I have tried to give the actual words used by the children themselves.

The play *The King Who couldn't stop Sneezing* arose out of the dramatisation of a story. As you will see, few characters have any more than a couple of lines to say, and even these may be omitted if the children have poor linguistic ability. In this case, the narrator can simply add the missing information while the children mime the actions. It is unlikely that you will have trouble in finding a king to do the sneezing. I have found that all the children tend to be keen to take this part, and I remember one occasion when this led to the play being done with *three* kings, all of whom had a birthday on the same day. Very few costumes are needed for this play, and there is no need for a set. It is a help if the children can have some real props to work with, for example, the cake, the cloak, the medicine bag and stethoscope for the doctor, etc., none of which are difficult to mock-up using cardboard, tissue and other scrap materials. For the trumpets use painted cardboard tubes or toy ones. There is no need to stick to the characters given in the script. Other characters can be added or substituted to suit the size and ability of the group.

The play set under the sea, *Michael's Midnight Adventure*, is one which arose out of music and movement work based on a sea theme. Although I have used the basis of this play quite a lot as class work, only one group of children have presented it in public. This was a mixed group of mentally and physically handicapped children. Most of the children in the group had reasonably good speech. The octopi were all wheelchair children. They were dressed in green crêpe paper, and the extra arms of the octopi were old tights, stuffed with paper, painted green and tied to the tops and sides of their chairs. For the dance, the children wheeled their chairs in formation. The percussion instruments were tied to trays in front of their chairs. This left their hands free to operate the chairs or the instruments as necessary. All of the other dance work was done by mobile children, while King Neptune was another physically handicapped, but not chairbound child. Again, the items in the cabaret can be added to or changed at will, depending on the size and ability of the group. As this particular group of children were also quite keen on singing, the song of the waves involved a number of sea shanties which the music teacher had rehearsed with them as part of their normal music lessons.

King George and the Dragon and *The Three Little Pigs* are both adapted from traditional tales. As both of these were on tape, the scripts given are an actual transcript of the tape, with no alteration. The *King George* script was developed by a group of mildly handicapped boys aged between ten and twelve. They performed it as part of the entertainment at a Christmas party for the younger children in the school. Most of the puppets were rod puppets, and the dragon was a long green sock, suitably 'dragonised' with the addition of egg box tops painted green. As the boys found it difficult to say words and operate the puppets at the same time, we taped the dialogue bit by bit in class as they worked on it. The tape was then played back as they operated the puppets. This is a fairly advanced play for mentally handicapped pupils, but the boys in this group had had a great deal of practice in classroom drama, and were very familiar with improvisation and dramatisation techniques. As a result, and because of the slow pace of the work, the development and taping of the dialogue presented them with few problems. With a less experienced group the dialogue evolved would, almost certainly, be less sophisticated.

The Three Little Pigs was developed as a radio play, and another group of children were invited to come into the classroom to listen to it. The group who developed the play were fairly young, and the play itself was built up with a minimum of speech and plenty of percussion and vocal 'noise' in the background. As the children in the group were linguistically poor, this provided an ideal medium for them to develop their vocal abilities, without placing a strain on their ability to use speech and language in a structured way. This tape was used subsequently by an older group of pupils as the background for a puppet play. Again, this was performed as part of a Christmas entertainment for the younger children.

THE KING WHO COULDN'T STOP SNEEZING

NARRATOR: It was the King's birthday. The Royal
            Cook had made a big birthday cake with

fifty candles on it. *(Enter cook with the cake.)* The Royal Maid had polished up the King's crown so it shone as brightly as when it was new. *(Enter maid with the crown.)* The Royal Trumpeters had written a new tune especially for the King on his birthday. *(Enter trumpeters to the accompaniment of taped music, they pretend to play a fanfare.)* And the Royal Dressmaker had made the King a brand new velvet cloak, trimmed with white feathers *(fur)* all round the neck. *(Enter dressmaker with the cloak.)* Then the King came in. All the people bowed before the King. *(King walks round as the people all bow or curtsey. Then the King takes his place on a throne centre stage.)* The Royal Dressmaker stepped forward.

DRESSMAKER:	For you, your Majesty. Happy Birthday. *(Dressmaker helps King to put on cloak, smoothing it out, etc.)*
KING:	Why, thank you, my dear.
NARRATOR:	Then the Royal Maid stepped forward.
MAID:	Happy Birthday, your Majesty. *(Steps forward to present the crown, giving it a final polish, etc.)*
NARRATOR:	But before the King could say thank you, he began to sneeze.
KING:	Achoo. Achoo. A-a-achoo.
NARRATOR:	The Royal Cook stepped forward. *(Cook brings cake, with much ooing and ahing from others, etc.)*
COOK:	Happy Birthday, your Majesty.
NARRATOR:	But before the King could say thank you, he began to sneeze.
KING:	Achoo. Achoo. A-a-achoo.
NARRATOR:	The Royal Trumpeters stepped forward. *(Trumpeters come forward and begin to play a*

fanfare to taped music.)
But before the King could say thank you he began to sneeze again.

KING: Achoo, achoo, achoo.

NARRATOR: He sneezed and he sneezed. *(While the King is sneezing and making a fuss, others react with consternation, etc.)*

KING: Achoo, achoo, achoo.

QUEEN: Oh, dear, the King has caught a cold. Send for the Royal Doctor.

ALL: Send for the Royal doctor. *(Trumpeters play till he comes.)*

DOCTOR: What's wrong, your Majesty?

KING: Achoo, achoo, achoo. *(Doctor makes great show of examining him, sounding his chest, etc. All look concerned and react appropriately.)*

DOCTOR: Oh dear, the King needs some medicine. Send for the Royal Chemist.

ALL: Send for the Royal Chemist. *(Trumpeters play while he comes.)*

CHEMIST: Drink this, your Majesty. This will make you better.
(The King drinks the medicine. All say 'Ah'. The King says 'Ah', then he begins to sneeze again. All say 'Oh'.)

QUEEN: Who can help the King?

JUGGLER: Let me try. *(Juggler juggles – all wait – then the King sneezes again. All say 'Oh'.)*

CLOWN: Let me try. *(Clown does funny tricks. All the people clap and laugh – then wait. The King sneezes again. All say 'Oh')*

DRESSMAKER: I have an idea. Your Majesty, give me your cloak.

KING: My – achoo – achoo – my cloak?

DRESSMAKER: Yes, your Majesty.

KING: Oh – achoo – very well. *(He gives her the cloak. The Dressmaker takes it to the centre and with a great flourish tears all the feathers (fur) off the cloak. All gasp, and say 'oh'. The King begins to roar. Then he stops. He smiles.)* I'm not sneezing any more.

ALL: He's cured. The King is cured. Hooray.

KING: I'm not sneezing any more.

DRESSMAKER: No, your Majesty. You see, your Majesty – it was the royal feathers *(fur)* on your royal cloak. It was tickling your royal nose.

KING: Tickling my royal nose. Tickling my royal nose. Why . . . ha, ha, ha – it was tickling my royal nose. *(He begins to laugh loudly. All begin to laugh too.)*

NARRATOR: And so the King was able to enjoy his birthday after all.
(Mime of King cutting his cake, everyone having a slice, drinking, his health, etc, Finish will all singing Happy Birthday.)

MICHAEL'S MIDNIGHT ADVENTURE

NARRATOR: Once there was a boy called Michael. One night when Michael was fast asleep a strange thing happened to him.
(Michael lying asleep in bed. Cat comes in and sits on the foot of his bed.)

CAT: Miaow.

MICHAEL: What was that?

CAT: Miaow.

MICHAEL: Oh, it's a cat. Who are you?

CAT: My name is Asparagus, but you can call me Gus, for short.

MICHAEL: But how did you get here?

CAT: I'm a magic cat. I can take you on a adventure.

MICHAEL: What kind of adventure?

CAT: Any kind you like. Tell me where you want to go.

MICHAEL:	To the bottom of the sea.
CAT:	Close your eyes and count to three
	Take my paw and follow me
	And I will take you to the bottom of the sea.
	(Michael follows the cat out. The scene changes to the bottom of the sea. If working in the round or in a classroom have part of the area set up as the bottom of the sea.)
MICHAEL:	Where am I?
CAT:	At the bottom of the sea, of course. Come with me.
	(Michael and Gus make their way over to where King Neptune sits, surrounded by people fanning him, serving him food, etc.)
KING:	Welcome, Michael. Welcome to my sea kingdom. Come, sit by me. Bring forth the banquet. *(Sound of gong. Music. Maidens bring in the banquet.)*
SERVANT:	*(Bangs on the gong.)* The dance of the eels. *(Music – the eels come in and dance to the music.)*
	(Bangs on the gong.) The octopus band. *(Musical backing while the octopi accompany this with percussion instruments.)*
	(Bangs on the gong) The duel of the swordfish. *(Music and mock sword fight)*
	(Bangs on the gong) The song of the waves. *(Waves make waving movements – either moving around or from a kneeling position. Musical backing while waves sing 'ah' to the music.)*
KING:	Did you enjoy that, Michael?
MICHAEL:	Oh yes. Thank you.
KING:	Would you like to see my treasure chest now?
MICHAEL:	Oh yes please.
KING:	Bring forth my treasure. *(Servant bangs on*

gong and maidens bring in treasure.)
You see, Michael. All the treasures of the sea. Pick them up. *(Michael doesn't pick up glittering 'stones'. He holds up pebbles.)*

MICHAEL: But look. They've turned into pebbles.

KING: Yes. When any human hand touches them they turn into pebbles.

MICHAEL: Look at this one. It's a funny shape. But it's very pretty even as a pebble.

KING: Keep it with you, Michael. It will remind you of us. But now you must go home.

CAT: Yes, time to go home, Michael.
Close your eyes and count to three
Take my paw and come with me
And I will take you home from the sea.
(Michael does so and follows the cat. He gets back into bed and the cat leaves.)

FATHER: Come on, Michael. Wake up. It's morning.

MICHAEL: Oh, I had a very funny dream.

FATHER: Hurry up and get dressed. You'll be late for school. Ouch.
(He stands on the pebble which has dropped to the floor by the bed.) I wonder where this came from? I've never seen a pebble like this before.

MICHAEL: Maybe it came from the bottom of the sea.

FATHER: What? Oh, yes. Maybe it did. *(He goes off and calls back.)*
Hurry up and get dressed, Michael. Come on.

MICHAEL: I'm coming. *(He looks at pebble and holds it up to the light. Then he calls out softly.)*
Thank you, Gus. *(He goes off. As he leaves we hear a soft 'miaow'. Then silence.)*

KING GEORGE AND THE DRAGON

KING: I am King Charles. I'm very brave. And I

	have killed many fierce animals. And I have even killed a dragon.
SERVANT:	King Charles, King Charles, there's a dragon outside.
KING:	A dragon!
SERVANT:	And it's breathing fire.
KING:	Breathing fire?
SERVANT:	Yes, and it's going to eat you up.
KING:	Eat me up? Help, help! Oooooooh.
SERVANT:	Surely you're not afraid, your Majesty.
KING:	Yes. I mean no. Certainly not.
SERVANT:	Well, I'm afraid. Help, help. *(He runs off. Dragon roars loudly offstage.)*
KING:	Did you hear that? *(Dragon roars offstage and red streamers are flicked up to look like fire.)*
KING:	Did you see that? *(Dragon roars again.)*
KING:	Oh, what am I going to do? Ah, I know what to do. Hide. Will you please not tell the dragon where I am. *(He hides.)*
DRAGON:	*(Roaring)* Where is he? Where is he? I am going to eat him up. *(Roar)* I can smell him, but I can't see him. Where is he? *(Roar)* Where is he? Where is he? Ah. *(Roars from dragon; shouts of help from King. King is chased by dragon until finally the king runs off.)*
DRAGON:	He got away that time but not the next time. When I get him I'm going to eat him. Ha, ha, ha! *(Dragon roars and exits. Enter King with servant.)*
KING:	H-has the d-d-dragon g-gone?
SERVANT:	Yes, your Majesty.
KING:	Thank goodness.
SERVANT:	Have you killed the dragon, your Majesty?

KING: Yes. And – no.

SERVANT: What do you mean, your Majesty. Yes or
                 no?

KING: Well I saw the dragon. And I pulled out
                 my sword. And I . . .
                 (Dragon roars offstage.)

SERVANT: The dragon's back again, your Majesty.
                 I'm off.
                 (Dragon roars offstage and says 'where is he?'
                 King runs and hides; enter dragon.)

DRAGON: Where is he? Where is he? That way?
                 That way – that way? Bah. I'll get him yet.
                 (Roars and then sees King. Repeat chase as
                 before but both King and dragon exit. Enter
                 Servant and nobles.)

SERVANT: Here is a message from King Charles of
                 England. Any man who can kill the
                 dragon will marry the king's beautiful
                 daughter.

CROWD: Hurray.

NOBLEMAN 1:   I will do it. I will kill the dragon. *(Dragon*
                 roars off.) Here he comes. *(Enter dragon*
                 roaring.) He's very big. *(Roar)* And he's
                 very fierce . . .

DRAGON: And I'm very hungry. *(Roars and chase as*
                 before and exit.)

NOBLEMAN 2:   Where's the dragon? I'm here to kill him.
                 (Dragon roars and enters.) Oh he's very big.
                 (roar) And he's very fierce . . .

DRAGON: And I am hungry *(roar)*.

NOBLEMAN 2:   I don't think I want to marry the King's
                 daughter. *(Roar)* Good boy. Good
                 dragon. Nice dragon. Nice dragon. Good
                 dragon. *(Roar)* Help!
                 (Chase as before. At the end of the chase all
                 exeunt. Enter the Princess, followed shortly
                 after by St George. The Princess is sobbing
                 loudly.)

GEORGE:	What's wrong?
PRINCESS:	The fierce dragon is here. And I have to marry the man who kills it (sobs).
GEORGE:	What's the matter with that?
PRINCESS:	I don't want to marry a soldier. I want to marry a Prince.
GEORGE:	But you must do what your father tells you.
PRINCESS:	Yes.
GEORGE:	Tell me about the dragon.
PRINCESS:	It's very big.
GEORGE:	So?
PRINCESS:	It's fierce.
GEORGE:	That doesn't bother me.
PRINCESS:	It breathes fire.
GEORGE:	That doesn't bother me either.
PRINCESS:	It's killed two soldiers and all the guards.
GEORGE:	It must be big. You go and lock yourself in the high tower. Maybe a soldier will come and kill the dragon.
PRINCESS:	I don't want to marry a soldier. I want to marry a Prince. (Roaring off) The dragon!
GEORGE:	Go quickly and lock yourself in the high tower.
PRINCESS:	Are you not coming?
GEORGE:	No. I'll stay here.
PRINCESS:	You watch yourself then. (Exit. Dragon roars. George goes off and comes back with a soldier's tunic on.)
GEORGE:	I have disguised myself as a soldier. Now I will kill the dragon and marry the Princess. (He hides.)
DRAGON:	Where is he, where is he? I can smell him but I can't see him. Where is he, where is he? (Roars)
GEORGE:	Here I am.
	(Sword fight between George and the dragon, George say 'Ah, ah,' etc. as he wields his

sword. Dragon roaring. Eventually George is the winner. Enter crowd, King, etc.)

CROWD: Hurray.

VOICE 1: The soldier has killed the dragon.

VOICE 2: The fierce dragon is dead.

VOICE 3: The dragon is dead.

CROWD: Hurray.

KING: You shall marry my beautiful daughter, and you shall become King of England. *(Crowd cheers)*

PRINCESS: I don't want to marry a soldier. I want to marry a Prince.

GEORGE: You'll just have to do what your father tells you.

PRINCESS: I'm sure I've heard that voice before.

GEORGE: Then will you marry me? A poor soldier like me?

PRINCESS: I must. My father made a promise.

GEORGE: Then you will be my bride. *(Cheers.)* You promised to marry a soldier. But wait here. *(Goes off and removes tunic.)* Look. *(Gasps and cries from crowd.)*

VOICE 1: It's Saint George.

VOICE 2: Saint George. *(Other voices take this up and repeat it.)*

ALL: Long live Saint George. *(Cheers.)*

VOICE: Saint George the dragon slayer. *(Cheers.)*

VOICE: Long live Saint George. *(Cheers.)*

SERVANT: And so Saint George the dragon killer shall live happily ever after with the Princess. *(Cheers.)*

THE THREE LITTLE PIGS

(Music – bring up to loud, then fade to off)

NARRATOR: We present – The Three Little Pigs. *(Bring up music then fade to off)*

NARRATOR: Once upon a time there were three little pigs. The first was called Squeaky.

SQUEAKY: Eeek, eek.

NARRATOR: The second was called Grunty.

GRUNTY: Grunt, grunt.

NARRATOR: And the third was called Porker.

PORKER: Oik, oik.

NARRATOR: One day the three little pigs were walking through the forest. (*Fingers tapped on desks to make sounds of footsteps; paper rustled and fingers flicked to make sounds of leaves crackling, etc.*) And the wind started to blow. (*Blowing and 'oo' sounds varying in loudness.*) It began to rain. (*Peas rolled backwards and forwards on a tray and maraccas shaken.*) The wind blew so hard that the three little pigs decided it was time they made a house. They stopped. (*Stop sound effects*) And the first little pig said:

SQUEAKY: I will build my house with straw.

NARRATOR: So the three little pigs set to work and began to build the house of straw.

ALL: (*singing to the tune of* Who's afraid of the big bad wolf?)
We will build a house of straw, a house of straw, a house of straw,
We will build a house of straw, ha, ha, ha, ha, ha.
(*the song is repeated twice. During the song various banging, tapping and rattling noises are made to represent the building.*)

NARRATOR: When the house was built the first little pig sat down in his house and prepared to spend the night there. The other two little pigs walked off through the forest. (*Footsteps and rustling leaves.*) But the wind began to blow again. (*Wind.*) And the rain came down. (*Sound of rain.*) And the rain fell harder. (*Louder rain.*) And the wind blew stronger. *(Louder wind.)* Until the two little pigs ran under a tree and stopped there for shelter. *(Sound of footsteps etc, become softer and then stop. Wind and rain gradually stop.)* And the second little pig said:

GRUNTY: I will build my house with sticks.

NARRATOR: So they set to work and began to build the house with sticks.

ALL: We will build a house of sticks, a house of sticks, a house of sticks,
We will build a house of sticks, ha, ha, ha, ha, ha.
(During the song repeat the building sounds, adding buzzing and rasping sounds for saw etc.)

NARRATOR: And when the house was built the second little pig got into his house and sat down, and prepared to spend the night there. But the third little pig continued on through the forest. *(Footsteps.)* And now the storm was very bad indeed. The wind blew *(Wind)* and the rain fell *(Rain)* and the leaves were crackling *(rustles)* and the branches of the trees were swaying and creaking in the wind. *(Hissing and squeaking sounds along with other sounds.)* And the little pig decided he must shelter for the night. And so the third little pig stopped. *(Gradually stop the effects.)* And he said . . .

PORKER: I will build my house of bricks.

NARRATOR: And he set to to build his little house of bricks.

ALL: We will build a house of bricks, a house of bricks, a house of bricks,
We will build a house of bricks, ha, ha, ha, ha, ha.

(During this song much louder and more rhythmic tapping and banging sounds.)

NARRATOR: And when he had finished he sat down in his little house and felt well pleased with himself. Now through the forest there came the sound of large footsteps. *(Tapping the desks with the flat of the hand and rustling kitchen foil.)* It was the wolf! He came to the house of the first little pig and he called in a very sweet voice:

WOLF: Little pig, little pig, let me in.

NARRATOR: But the first little pig said . . .

SQUEAKY: No.

NARRATOR: So the big bad wolf said . . .

WOLF: I'll huff and I'll puff and I'll blow your house down.

NARRATOR: So he huffed *(Sounds of blowing)* and he puffed *(Blowing.)* And he blew the house down. *(Sounds to represent the falling of the house.)* The first little pig ran to the house of his brother *(quick footsteps – fingers tapping lightly.)* And the big bad wolf ran behind him. *(Quick footsteps – flat of hand tapped more loudly.)* And the first little pig ran into his brother's house and shut the door. *(Ruler rapped on table.)* And when the big bad wolf came to the house of the second little pig he rapped on the door *(Sounds of knocking)* and he said . . .

WOLF: Little pig, little pig, let me in.

NARRATOR: But the two little pigs said . . .

PIGS: No.

NARRATOR: So the big bad wolf said . . .

WOLF: Then I'll huff and I'll puff and I'll blow your house down.

NARRATOR: So he huffed *(Blow)*, and he puffed *(Blow)*, and he huffed *(Blow)* and he puffed *(Blow)* and he blew the house down. (*Clatter of house falling. Sounds of footsteps as before.*) The two little pigs ran as fast as they could to the house of their brother. And the big bad wolf followed on with big, big steps. When the two little pigs reached their brother's house of bricks, they ran in and shut the door. (*Slam.*) But the big bad wolf knocked on the door (*Knocking*) and said:

WOLF: Little pig, little pig, let me in.

NARRATOR: But the three little pigs said . . .

PIGS: No.

NARRATOR: So the big bad wolf said . . .

WOLF: I'll huff and I'll puff and I'll blow your house down.

NARRATOR: So he huffed (*Blow*), and he puffed (*Blow*), and he huffed, and he puffed, and he huffed and he puffed and he huffed and he puffed (*Loud blowing throughout*) and he grew so tired that he fell down. (*Thump.*) He couldn't blow down the little house of bricks. The three little pigs said . . .

PIGS: Hurray.

NARRATOR: And the big bad wolf said . . .

WOLF: Bah . . . bah.

NARRATOR: And he ran off through the forest. (*Sounds of footsteps fading.*) And was never seen again.
And so the three little pigs, Squeaky . . .

SQUEAKY: EEEk, eeek.

NARRATOR: Grunty . . .

GRUNTY: Grunt, grunt

NARRATOR: . . . and Porker . . .

PORKER: Oik, oik.

NARRATOR: . . . lived happily ever after in the little house of bricks. And every day they sang . . .

PIGS: We're not afraid of the big bad wolf, the
                         big bad wolf, the big bad wolf,
                         We're not afraid of the big bad wolf, ha,
                         ha, ha, ha, ha.

(Bring up music then fade to off.)

Classified Bibliography

General Books on Drama in Education

Adland, D.E., *Group Drama*, Longmans, 1964.

Allen, J., *Drama in Schools; Its Theory and Practice*, Heinemann, 1979.

Bolton, G., *Towards a Theory of Drama in Education*, Longmans, 1980.

Courtney, R., *Teaching Drama*, Cassell, 1964.

Courtney, R., *The School Play*, Cassell, 1966.

Courtney, R., *Play, Drama and Thought*, Cassell, 1974.

Hodgson, J. & Banham, M., *Drama in Education*, Vols. 1, 2 & 3, Pitman, 1972–5.

McCaslin, N., *Children and Drama*, David McKay, New York, 1975.

McGregor, L., Tate, M., & Robinson, K., *Learning Through Drama*, Heinemann Educational, 1977.

Slade, P., *Child Drama*, University of London Press, 1954.

Stabler, T., *Drama in Primary Schools*, Macmillan Educational, 1978.

Way, B., *Development through Drama*, Longmans, 1967.

Drama in the Education of Mentally Handicapped People

Heathcote, D., 'Drama and Education; Subject or System' in *Drama and Theatre in Education*, Dodd, N. & Hickson, W. (eds), Heinemann Educational, 1971.

Heathcote, D., 'Drama as Challenge' in *The Uses of Drama*, Hodgson, J. (ed), Eyre Methuen, 1972.

Hudson, J., & Slade, P., *A Chance for Everyone*, Cassell, 1968.

Jennings, S., *Creative Therapy*, Pitman, 1975.

Jennings, S., *Remedial Drama*, Pitman, 1973.

Lord, G. (ed), *The Arts and Disabilities*, Macdonald, 1981.

Upton, G. (ed), *Physical and Creative Activities for the Mentally Handicapped*, Cambridge University Press, 1979.

Source Material for Themes

Beginning to Learn Series, published by Blackwell Raintree (*subjects covered include colours, hearing, shapes, opposites, etc.*).

Easy-Read Holiday Books Series, published by Franklin Watts (*good source of background ideas for Christmas, Easter, Hallowe'en, etc.*).

Learning Library Series, published by Blackwell (*over a hundred subjects covered, good source of pictures for stimulus or illustrating a theme*).

Topic Books Series, published by Macdonald (*good source of background information on pirates, castles, jungles, farms, witches and wizards, circus, etc.*).

The Starters Series, published by Macdonald (*excellent illustrations for people who help us, shape, colour, circus, maths, etc. Over seventy topics covered*).

Theories of Play and Play Activities

Bruner, J., *Play: Its Role in Development and Evolution*, Penguin, 1976.

Jeffree, D., McConkey, R., & Hewson, S., *Let me Play*, Souvenir Press, 1977.

Kiernan, C., Jordan, R., & Saunders, C., *Starting Off*, Souvenir Press, 1978.

Manning, K., & Sharp, A., *Structuring Play in the Early Years*, Ward Lock, 1977.

Matterson, E. M., *Play With a Purpose for the Under Sevens*, Penguin, 1970.

Miller, S., *The Psychology of Play*, Penguin, 1969.

Owen, D., *Play Games*, Muller, 1977.

Mime, Movement and Speech Activities

Bruce, V. R., *Dance and Drama in Education*, Pergamon Press, 1966.

Bruford, R., *Teaching Mime*, Methuen, 1958.

Jeffree, D. M., & McConkey, R., *Let Me Speak*, Souvenir Press, 1976.

Keysell, P., *Motives for Mime*, Evans, 1975.

Levete, G., *No Handicap to Dance*, Souvenir Press, 1982.

Sansom, C., *Acting Rhymes* (Bks. 1 & 2), A. C. Black, 1959.

Sansom, C., *Speech Rhymes* (Bks. 1 & 2), A. C. Black, 1959.

Sherbourne, V., 'Movement as a Preparation for Drama' in *Drama and Theatre in Education*, Dodd, N. & Hickson, W. (eds), Heinemann, 1971.

Wethered, A. C., *Drama and Movement in Therapy*, Macdonald & Evans, 1973.

Wiles, J., & Garrard, A., *Leap to Life*, Chatto & Windus, 1965.

Role-Play, Dramatic Play and Improvisation

Casciani, J. W., & Watt, I., *Drama in the Primary School*, Nelson, 1966.

Hodgson, J., & Richards, E., *Improvisation*, Methuen, 1966.

Slade, P., *Experience in Spontaneity*, Longmans, 1968.

Short Action Rhymes and Poems

Carrick, M., *All Sorts of Everything*, Heinemann, 1973.

Edwards, R., *Let's Enjoy Poetry*, Dent, 1959.

Heseler, A., *Off and Away Rhymes for the Nursery*, Dent, 1979.

Reeves, J., *The Christmas Book*, Heinemann, 1968.

Simpson, C., *Lucky Dip*, Angus & Robertson, 1970.

Puppetry

Astell-Burt, C., *Puppetry for Mentally Handicapped People*, Souvenir Press, 1981.

Brody, V., & Heron, M. F., *Puppets and Hand Games*, Collins, 1974.

Dean, A. W., *Puppets that are Different*, Faber and Faber, 1973.

Jenkins, P. G., *The Magic of Puppetry*, Prentice-Hall, New York, 1980.

Simple Plays

Barter, N., *Playing with Plays*, Macdonald , 1979.

Cochrane, L., *Tabletop Theatres and Plays*, Chatto & Windus, 1973.

Hawkesworth, *Rag Picture Shows*, Faber & Faber, 1974.

Dramatisation

Althea, *The School Fair*, Dinosaur Publications, 1982.

East, H., *Michael Goes Shopping*, Macdonald, 1981.

Fitch, J., *Story-telling for Slow Learning Children*, National Council for Special Education, 1974.

Gage, W., *Mrs Gaddy and the Ghost*, Bodley Head, 1979.

Murphy, J., *Peace at Last*, Macmillan Children's Books, 1981.
Hynds, M., *The Wishing Bottle*, Blackie, 1975.
Proysen, A., *Mrs Pepperpot's Christmas*, Puffin, 1981.
Reeves, J., *Eggtime Stories*, Blackie, 1978.
Roberts, E., *All About Simon and his Grandmother*, Puffin, 1975.
Russell, J., *The Man from Mars*, Blackie, 1972.
Waters, F., *Playtime Reading with Mother*, Harrap, 1979.
Wilson, P. M., *Katie Goes to Hospital*, Angus & Robertson, 1981.

Useful Records
Atwell, Winifred, *More, More Piano*.
Anderson, Leroy, *Conducts his own Compositions*.
Clayderman, Richard, *16 Grandes Temas de Siempre*.
Debussy, *Golliwog's Cakewalk*.
Delibes, *Coppelia*.
Dukas, *Sorcerer's Apprentice*.
Dvorak, *New World Symphony*.
Emerson, Lake & Palmer, *Triology*.
Grieg, *Peer Gynt Suites 1 & 2*.
Holst, *The Planets Suite*.
Boulevard Records, *Honky Tonk Selection*.
Lennon, John, *Mind Games*.
Mrs Mills, *Non-stop Honky Tonk Party*.
Pink Floyd, *The Wall*.
Saens-Sens, *Carnival of the Animals*.
Simon & Garfunkel, *Bridge Over the Genius of Simon and Garfunkel*.
Wagner, Adrian, *Instincts*.

Some Useful Contacts

The British Association of Drama Therapists, 7 Hatfield Road, St. Albans, Herts.
   (Publications and conferences on drama therapy.)
British Institute for the Study of the Arts in Therapy (also Sesame), Christchurch, 27 Blackfriars Road, London SE1 8NY.
   (Publications, workshops and performances arranged for schools, hospitals, etc.)
Cockpit Theatre and Arts Workshop, Gateforth Street, Marylebone, London, NW1.
The Drama Board and Central Council for Amateur Theatre, PO Box 44, Banbury, Oxon OX15 4EQ.
   (Advice on all matters concerning amateur drama.)
Drama with the Blind, Advisory Group, c/o Royal National Institute for the Blind, 224/8 Great Portland Street, London W1N 6AA.
The Educational Drama Association, Vauxhall Gardens School, Barrack Street, Birmingham B7 4HA.
   (Publications and advice on drama in education, and drama with handicapped people.)
Interim Theatre Company Limited, 3 Spring Lane, London SE25 4SP.
   (Information on drama and theatre for deaf people.)
National Association for Drama in Education and Children's Theatre (also National Council of Theatre for Young People), c/o British Theatre Centre, 9 Fitzroy Square, London W1P 6AE.
   (Advice and information broadsheets.)
Centre of the Environment for the Handicapped, Penny Smith (information officer), 126 Albert Street, London NW1 7NF.
   (Information broadsheet on all forms of play provision for the mentally handicapped.)

Playspace, c/o Polytechnic of Central London, 309 Regent Street, London W1R 8AL.

(Judy Ryde, organiser of drama performances and workshops.)

The Educational Puppetry Association, Puppet Centre, c/o Battersea Arts Centre, Lavender Hill, London SW11 5JT.

The Scottish Mime Theatre, 36a Lauriston Place, Edinburgh EH3 9EZ.

(Drama for the deaf.)

Ms Seona Reid, Director, Shape, 7 Fitzroy Square, London W1P 6AE.

(Information, advice and workshops on all aspects of the arts and handicap.)

The Workshop, 34 Hamilton Place, Edinburgh EH3 5AX.

(Training workshops in all aspects of the arts.)